D1541985

THE ULTIMATE REVOLUTION

THE ULTIMATE

REVOLUTION

Introducing the Now Age

Walter Starcke

Published by
GUADALUPE PRESS

ISBN:0-929845-05-6

Library of Congress Catalog Card Number 88-072196

"Now learn a parable of the fig tree: When his branch is yet tender, and putteth forth leaves ye know that summer is nigh: So likewise ye, when ye shall see all these things, know that it is near, even at the doors. Verily I say unto you, This generation shall not pass, till all these things be fulfilled."

Matthew 24:32–35

The English language doesn't seem to be ready for unisex pronouns, and the singular form often says it better and is less awkward than the "he or she" game. My intentions are good, so though I use an occasional mixture of genders, in any case I am referring to the One being we all are.

Contents

Author's Note   9
  1. How It Was   17
  2. Off With Their Heads   32
  3. The Morality of Grace   44
  4. The Identity Dilemma   72
  5. The Necessity of Others   96
  6. Contact Morality   114
  7. The Puzzle of Sex and Drugs   133
  8. The Meditation Miracle   158
  9. The Healing Spirit   181
 10. The Ultimate Trip   201

Author's Note

It's easy to say, "Don't judge by appearances," or "Think positively," and any of us who have tried to live the so-called spiritual life have felt either guilty or angry over our unsuccessful attempts to do so. Just about the time we believe that a new order has finally arrived something happens that makes us believe we have been kidding ourselves. Nevertheless that is just what I am saying—don't judge by appearances, the day we have been waiting for is here.

However disturbing or tragic the present conflicts appear to be, they contain nothing that should shake the foundations of our faith in the future. Though a relatively few isolated human beings might falter, the sum total of the collective consciousness cannot fail to find its union and its God.

Just think of it, for hundreds of millions of years consciousness has been constantly rising up to the surface of human awareness. What makes us think that the direction of this tremendous current of human evolution will reverse itself at the very time when we are now beginning to realize its reality.

Without a doubt, this last decade of the 20th century is shaping up to be the most remarkable, if not the most tumultous, possibly frightening, and revolutionary one the world has ever seen. Mark my word. By the time this roller coaster decade is over, a profound sense of urgency to form one single body coexistent with itself and of a collective responsibility to that body will have transformed the lives of everyone on earth and will have linked all peoples into a world family. As a result there will be one recognizable economy, the resources of our planet will be shared, wars will, thank God, be a thing of the past, and instead of trying to conquer each other, the world will be united to triumph over a common enemy—waste and pollution.

The pendulum always swings before it settles down; there will be times when our two steps forward will be obscured by our one step back. The echos of past ignorances will tempt us to believe the world hasn't really changed. Localized wars, ethnic clashes, and erratic financial chaos will tempt us to doubt, but if we can see how different these current situations are in seemingly similar ones from the past we can get a fix on the larger picture. We can realize that our presently disturbing occasions are the scabs left over from the sores of our past spiritual diseases soon to be sloughed off.

The blood stream of global perception is undergoing a purifying shift in consciousness. What is taking place now is a divine tug of war for the completion and stewardship of the earth. We are making a giant step forward. Though disturbances will be evident as the cleansing process continues, this decade will come to be recognized as the Now Age. With its advent what we have called the New Age will become an anacronism. We will see that the New Age we have sought to achieve is here now. When we dissolve fear and no longer deny its arrival by continuing to think of it as yet to come we will be aware that this is the decade of the Now Age.

For that matter, a decade is a very short time. Many of us have already lived a number of them. When you stop to think of it, Jesus was born only 199 decades ago. That is yesterday rather than ancient history, and if you realize how far we have come since his birth, it is obvious that the revolution Jesus started has finally come into flower. This decade will see Christ consciousness blossom into universal awareness. It will take the next century for the full totalizing of the world, but this decade is ushering it in.

Spiritually, a revolution or turn-around does not result so much in destruction as in evolution. It represents an overturning or a shift in priorities. As nothing can be eliminated from the infinite nature of life, what has been of secondary value becomes primary. In the past, human rights, freedoms, and the desire of individuals to be included were sublimated to national and personal interests. Now a shift in values has taken place which, when the smoke clears, will reveal that those things which separated us from each other have lost their power due to the spiritual awakening of this Now Age.

The scriptural adage, "It is easier for a camel to go through the eye of a needle than for a rich man to enter into the kingdom of God" is still true; the rich nations will most likely be the last to capitulate to this shift in consciousness. If they cling to the old ways of thinking some world leaders may have to suffer the ignominy of defeat in order to get the point, but when the Berlin wall came down the New Age became the Now Age. Now, when old methods are employed, sooner or later the international outcry will demand new solutions. If we individually want to be on the side of the angels to the degree that we keep the faith and do not buy in to the old ways by being paranoid ourselves, we will help speed up the divine process.

What we must do is to look for differences. When before has the whole world been involved in or concerned about each other's local issues? When before have big changes anywhere come by shifts in consciousness rather than by force? When before have environmental issues even been discussed in a world forum? When before has the United Nations begun to act collectively and laid the foundation for each cooperation?

Sometimes looking back helps us better understand the present. It helps because a look at them and the differences puts today into perspective. I can well remember a time when we had to face many of the issues that are resurfacing today. No experience is wasted.

There were two events which took place over twenty years ago which symbolized the beginning of the revolution that is just now coming to its final climax. You might say those two events marked the birth of what has been called the New Age, the age which has led to this Now Age. The first event was the historic rock concert which took place at Woodstock, New York where for the first time thousands upon thousands of young people drew together as if by some hidden signal to a countryside meadow in order to listen to music, rejoice in a feeling of oneness, and to open Pandora's box of psychedelic drugs. The minute those of us who had been on the path for years heard of it, we knew that Woodstock represented the advent of a new united state of consciousness. Our young were telling us something. They did not understand it themselves, but they knew that a new way for humankind to live together was coming about.

The other event which clearly announced the quality of that revolutionary beginning was the opening of the Broadway musical *Hair*. In what was then considered to be a shocking production, long-haired youths protested the Vietnamese war, lamented being misunderstood by their parents, called upon their fellow Americans to spurn the luxury of their backgrounds, to break with the establishment and to "drop out." They advocated the use of drugs to escape the mind, and stunned the critics by a climactic moment in the show where the whole cast stood facing the audience naked as jay birds—though the lights were discretely dimmed.

Those of us who had felt for years that a spiritual breakthrough was on the horizon joined the young in the celebration. With as much gusto as they, we sang the leading song from *Hair*, "This is the dawning of the age of Aquarius." But then we noticed that the flower children, as they were called, would rip each other off, and heard them use the words, "Do your own thing," as an excuse so that they themselves could be totally selfish or self-centered.

As war and chaos continued, and love was not so much practiced as talked about, I for one felt bitterly betrayed, even doubted my guidance which had told me a new age was being born. Fortunately, before too long I saw what was happening and the validity of my guidance has been vindicated over the years.

Whether that seemingly lost generation, born after the Second World War, was the karmic result of America's using the atom bomb, as some have claimed, or whether along with their ragged clothes, unwashed appearance, and spacey attitude they were the sacrificial lambs sent to usher in new values, is beside the point. The new Aquarian age consciousness was indeed born in 1969, but like all new babies it has taken years to raise it up through all the stages of growth into maturity. Now, twenty-one years later, it is literally coming of age.

This book, with a new introduction and slightly revised, was originally written to form a bridge between the rebellious young of that unique time and their bewildered parents and to offer some guidelines for living in the new age.

In those days, I had a home in Key West, Florida which became nationally known as a "hippie" hang-out. I spent hours on the beach with the kids in wide-ranging "rap" sessions. I got a number of them out of jail for vagrancy charges and, though I was not into drugs myself, sometimes I could be found reading the Bible to groups of hippies in some crash pad, thinking that at any minute the law would storm in, find some drugs, and take us all to jail. I could just see the headlines, "Religious author caught in drug bust." But I was also of the parent generation, so I felt I could see both sides of the situation. When the book came out, I received many letters from parents who had given it to their children and vice versa. For that I have always been grateful.

I am putting out this new edition for several reasons, partly because some of the same conditions that were taking place at that time are briefly occurring now as the pendulum makes one of its swings before it permanently settles down. By seeing where we have come from in the past 21 years, we can better understand where we are now. Also, I've had time to see how practical the guide lines set forth in the book for living in this Now Age have proved themselves. Another reason is because when I have been on the road, more people have told me they have received help from this book than from any of my others, and because in rereading it, I can see how far I have come myself and how truly prophetic the book has become.

Perhaps more importantly, this book can help us understand the spiritual nature of the disturbing events that are happening today along with the excitingly encouraging ones that proclaim the Now Age. It's still a bridge book, a bridge that can help us listen to God, ourselves and each other.

Perhaps most significantly of all, we can now see that the silence is broken. After centuries of loneliness and fear, we and our nations are starting to listen to one another. In our homes, we were pushed into listening by our young people because many of them were experimenting with dandies from the medicine cabinets powerful enough to transform them into strangers overnight. In our cities, we have been forced into listening because vandals have roamed the streets and pushers have hung around school yards. Internationally, we have been shoved into listening because nations have once more been playing with toys that can blow the world to bits or poison its air if we refuse to listen to each other. Listening is no longer a luxury; it is a necessity. We may have been scared into communicating, but I am nevertheless delighted that it is finally happening.

All of us, young and old, female or male, black and white and yellow and red, saint and sinner, are individual persons wanting, if not demanding, to be heard.

I myself, in my listening, have come to realize that every person I have ever encountered, from grocery clerk to clergyman, from the stranger I casually pass in a crowd to my most intimate companion, has helped me to grow into whatever I am today. Each of us affects the other. Because you are what you are, I am what I am. Because I am what I am, you are what you are. For that reason, I can say that I have not written this book—you have, or rather everyone who has ever lived has contributed to it. We have all written it for We are One. So go back in time with me and let us see what we have to say to each other.

CHAPTER ONE

How It Was

Back in the late nineteen sixties, I had a personal confrontation of agonizing proportions. I was out on the West Coast lecturing. For quite a while I had felt a pressure building up, a sense of frustration in trying to reconcile my naturally affirmative attitude toward life with a growing realization that revolution was part and parcel of that day. Like many others, I tried to turn my eyes away from signs of revolution. I wanted to push out negative or disruptive images, but it was becoming increasingly difficult.

One day a particularly full schedule of appointments brought me in contact with a wide variety of people. I heard all manner of problems, bitterness, and complaints from both those who were part of the so-called establishment and those who had left conventional life. I listened to people who were just plain paranoid, projecting their fears out onto everyone and everything they could. I listened to those who were on the side of the angels but who had also gotten caught up in fighting evil or projecting their fears onto society. I was struggling to keep my head above the onslaught of defeatism and the lack of confidence or self-love I saw people expressing. To top it all off, every headline seemed to scream hate and violence. The noise of our music, the look of our clothes, and the smell of our air reflected one thing: revolution. There was no escaping it.

When I got back to my hotel I locked myself in and started to meditate, listen, think, and call on every spiritual and intellectual truth I knew in order to clear my own confusion. As the young of that day would say, I was working hard trying to pull my head together. I had to. The chips were down. My belief in God was on the block.

A long time before then I had come to the conviction that I wasn't alive without a sense of God—a universal divine purpose behind life, some transcendental oneness. I knew that I needed a kind of infinite being-ness with which to relate in order to understand my own finite nature. I knew that anything worthy of being called God would have to be all-knowing, in all things, and all-powerful. So I had come to the conclusion that evil couldn't actually exist because we couldn't have God plus evil. If evil did exist, it had to be part of God, for God is everywhere and the only power. I realized that when I was strong enough to look at evil without fear and see what was behind it, I found out that either what appeared to be evil had a creative purpose or that it dissolved before my eyes as though I was waking from a bad dream.

It became apparent to me that those who were busily

fighting evil or sin had a concept of God that was different from mine. At least, if they were claiming that God was omnipresent, omniscient, and omnipotent, they were performing some fancy spiritual footwork in justifying those beliefs while at the same time resisting or fearing evil or sin.

That night in California I reminded myself of my beliefs. Then I measured the disturbing conditions that I was seeing in the world against those principles. At last the light broke and I got my head and spirit clear. What I saw was alarming at first. I saw a nation staggering under a loss of faith. The American dream had been built on our positive attitude, our self-confidence, our belief in our infallibility, our ability to overcome obstacles, our sense of justice, and our belief in God. Everywhere faith was collapsing like a house of cards.

Before the Vietnamese War, it was forgivable at one time or another to lose faith in most things, but it was unthinkable to lose faith in the United States itself. Now, however, great numbers were losing faith in the country. The older generation was confused and often tried to force faith on the young, but even the old timers' protestations of faith sounded as hollow as the forced flag-waving demonstration we see at a political convention. Finally it occurred to me what was behind this apparent loss of faith, and I could breathe again.

I saw that the tide of national, if not universal, loss of faith was good. It represented change. Whenever change takes place, faith in the old way has to give way for there to be faith in the new, in things more worthy of faith. Man once had faith that the world was flat, but when he found out it was round he lost faith in his flat world. Scientists tell us daily of discoveries that make old systems obsolete, causing us to lose faith in the old ways. Evolution, revolution, change. They are all part and parcel of the same thing, and we will probably continue this process of gaining and losing faith over and over until we grow into our full spiritual being.

I realized then that I was wrong in fearing revolution. Any desire I might have had to turn the clock back to the "good old days" came because I was frightened by change. I didn't want to retreat to the past; I wanted to get *away from* the present. I wanted to drop out. When I pictured revolutionaries only as characters from the television screen angrily rushing around tossing Molotov cocktails and spitting obscenities, I was missing the point. Anyone who was dedicated to faith in the future of humankind, anyone who was willing to change and grow, was a revolutionary.

I realized that the tricky thing about growth is that it always assumes the appearance of an act of destruction. If I build a house I have to cut down some trees to make lumber. If I have a root-bound garden it becomes necessary to dig up all the plants, fertilize, and reset them in order for the garden to grow to greater glory. Someone who walks in just when I have ripped up all the plants is bound to be alarmed—unless he or she has faith in the future.

Then it came to me. "The world is being dug up. All the separate little patches of self-interest, all the unrelated hodgepodge of confusion will, when the revolution is over, be assembled in one grand master plan resulting in a world more beautiful than I can imagine. All the hopes and dreams I have ever wanted for man, all the beautiful potential in the world, are ready to be fulfilled." I realized then that the fulfillment of this potential was what the revolution was really about.

In the meantime I had to tell myself not to be confused by the signs of violence and disruption. Instead of panicking I had to have enough faith to look right at the disturbances to see what they could tell me. I saw that behind each disturbing sign was the crumbling of a system that had tricked man into putting his faith in a host of such unworthy objects as money, guns, pills, material success, and tyranical leaders.

I looked at money. The financial revolution appeared in the form of an international monetary upheaval as nations politically manipulated currency. At home, taxes, insurance rates, and inflation made it increasingly impossible to hang on to personal wealth, thus forcing us to stop depending on money. I was amused to discover that in some of our poverty programs our government found it cheaper to give money away without checking on the validity of the individual claims than to finance the mountain of paperwork necessary for verifying claims. Trust was becoming an economic necessity. That's revolution.

When I looked at the disturbing signs of war, I realized that man had always put his trust in guns to get him what he wanted. But now the guns in our soldiers' hands were becoming obsolete, not because of more efficient weapons but because of the power of the will within people. Numerically smaller countries were managing to stand against much larger and better-armed forces because of the will of people for self-determination. At last, in some cases, right was becoming more powerful than might, and man was beginning to put his faith in right rather than in guns. That's revolution.

I looked at the disturbing reports stating that more of our hospital beds were filled with mental patients than with people suffering physical problems. Many of the nervous breakdowns were experienced by housewives and mothers who had placed their reliance on pills to keep them slimmed down and pepped up at the same time. Their pill prisons had alienated them from their own children and themselves. If it took a nervous breakdown to straighten out their false values and to teach them to place their faith in themselves, perhaps it was worth the price.

I looked at people who were pained to see their churches empty with the doors locked, to see their clubs unable to recruit new members, to see their governments unable to govern. Then it dawned on me that many of the systems were folding up because they had accomplished their purpose.

For instance, I heard complaints from those who were still trying to hang on to the old concept of church responsibility. They felt that the social welfare aims of their church in foreign and domestic fields were losing ground because the Peace Corps and government welfare programs were doing the job so much better than the church. They didn't realize that the church's failure was a sign of its success. For many years the church was the only body interested in the social welfare of backward nations and the underprivileged in our own nation. But finally the church had succeeded in breeding man's basic human responsibility to his fellow man into our national conscience, into our government. I realized that if the church would lead the way in finding new and better systems, it would be alive. Perhaps it had to be emptied out in order to be filled up with fresh air. That's revolution.

The game of finding God behind disturbing appearances went on and on. Sometimes it took a long time for me to "let go" of my old beliefs in order to find new ones. The hardest belief to let go of was the belief in *good*. It was much easier to stop seeing bad, was much easier to convince myself that I was being tricked by negative appearances, that something wasn't really bad, than it was to get over believing things were good. But I found out that I couldn't reconcile bad appearances with a God of one power until I went beyond both bad and good, until I forced myself to look at things without any opinion whatsoever. Every time I managed to reach that judgeless stage beyond good and evil, I found freedom and with it a growing excitement about the adventure of life.

Finally, I turned my attention to the student revolts that were taking place at that time. It seemed to me that the student revolution combined all aspects of the overall revolution. It was the very symbol of revolution.

Most of us instinctively want to have faith in the young. Our hopes have been pinned on the young; both their successes and their failures come to roost at our doorstep, for they are the product of the society we have fashioned in the past. Maybe that is why the older people get so upset when the young rebel. Then I realized that the young were bent on bringing into reality the world we taught them it was possible to have. They actually believed the American dream we talked about, only they saw no reason why it couldn't be a world dream for everyone, no matter what sex, color, or nationality. They may not have always used the right means to achieve their ends, but the ends they sought were noble ones. Those young people were our greatest successes. They were and are going to do what we dreamed of but failed to believe was really possible.

It came to me that the student revolt was hard to understand because students were revolting over something much deeper than easily comprehensible surface issues. They were fighting mainly to avoid being integrated into a society dominated by economic interests, a world whose techniques of brainwashing manipulated people and caused them to lose their sense of personal importance, reduced them in turn to grasping power-hungry machines designed to contribute more to perpetuating old systems than to the development of their individual selves. That was the key I was looking for—the importance of the individual.

Behind every aspect of the overall revolution there seem to be people who are waking up to an awareness of their personal self and its importance, most notably women who had been secondary citizens for so long.

When Malcolm X, the most outstanding revolutionary of that period, taught black people that they had been brainwashed out of realizing their true identity, he was speaking for all mankind, not just the black. Whatever our color, sex, nationality, size, or shape, we were *all* ignorant of our true identity and capacity, all faced with the problem of finding out who we really were. — God!

I realized that perhaps this problem would go on and on until we woke up to our own Godhood, to the actual fact that every single one of us is, as Paul said, "heir and joint heir with Christ in God"—not inferior to, not less than, but equal with, by nature of our Oneness.

I saw that everyone who refuses to give up his or her individual identity, who refuses to live in the service of any system which subordinates him or her, who refuses to be integrated into existing systems which lose sight of the importance of the individual, is a revolutionary proclaiming that the very foundation of our society is on trial.

I almost exploded when I realized how really wonderful that was. Always in the past we have busied ourselves putting salve on the individual sores of humanity. No sooner have we cured one trouble spot than another one has popped up. All the different signs of disruption and revolution were like individual sores on the body of mankind. We could go on forever fighting battle after battle, but if we want to put an end to sickness itself, sooner or later we have to cure the bloodstream. We have to get at the underlying cause. All the individual revolutions we were witnessing on the campuses, in the streets, in the laboratories, in every conceivable area of life, added up to one thing. Humanity was now refusing to live any longer by laws that dehumanize it. HUMANITY WAS COMING OF AGE. Humanity was finding out who it is, and it's wonderful to behold. Humanity was designed to be the perfect instrument to house the spirit, and when it is fully human it will be the embodiment of spirit. Humanity sees no reason to continue putting up with mental and physical sickness. It's going to rebel and rebel until the cause of revolution is eliminated.

The next thing I asked myself was: Then what law dehumanizes people? What single law has most brainwashed people? Right away it came to me how often I have heard people say, "Well, that's human nature," in order to excuse people's injustices and shortcomings. They say that the first law of human nature is survival, that people will always end up protecting themselves at everyone else's expense, that human nature is selfish, treacherous, and evil. That's the lie this revolution is out to expose, the lie that creates all duality. In a crowded world we no longer have space for the selfish interests of what we have been taught to believe was human nature. The revolution will go on until that law is broken. The funny thing is that the mystics have told us for years and years and years that we had to overcome the first law of human nature, but only now are we being forced into it.

Why now? was my next thought. Long before this I

had been convinced that everything appearing on earth was at its level of being as a process of evolution. I knew that human beings had taken countless centuries evolving into whatever they were at the moment, and each stage was necessary; people have always been evolving out of their animal background into their humanity. I thought, "Up to and including the present, people have been caught in the middle of the conflict between their animal instinct and their awakening spiritual instinct. As a matter of fact, individuals are body, mind, and spirit; all three aspects have been evolving, but perhaps the body aspect has developed in advance of the individual's mental and spiritual evolvement. At any rate, most of what we have called human nature has actually been the remains of animal nature from which people have not yet fully evolved. The problem isn't with "human nature." It is that we were just then becoming *fully human*. People will now shake off the yoke of the old law of human nature, for they are evolving into their "spiritual" humanity. Whenever I see anyone acting out of fear, injustice, or cruelty, I can remind myself not to blame human nature. Instead I can think, "Oh, he is still operating out of his subhuman nature." I realized that Jesus gave us the two commandments to love God and neighbor, the human being, and that when it was done they would be "like unto each other," so our humanity would be like our spirituality in the end when it was fully what humanity is for.

When I came to the realization that mankind in general was just now coming into the fullness of its humanity, some other very important pieces fell into place. During my life I have gone through the whole range of rejecting religion, then finding ways to reconcile it with my life; rejecting Jesus Christ, then finding what a remarkable light he was and what incredible secrets were hidden in his message. I finally realized that because mankind is the product of evolution there had to be some one man or woman who marked the advent of the first fully human being. If so, Jesus would represent that advent to the Western world and Buddha would to the East. No wonder the world instinctively worshiped these men. People knew Jesus and Buddha signified something profound that would one day be inherited by the whole of mankind. In fact, each of them taught, "Greater works will ye do." No wonder they, too, were considered to be revolutionaries. But more important, when I realized what these men represented in terms of evolution and that humankind was beginning to catch up with their evolved consciousnesses, I knew that it applied to me as well as others, that perhaps I, too, was growing into my Christhood or Buddhahood.

By this time, as you can see, I was ready to fly. I was ready to run up and down the streets shouting, "Ring the bells! Throw confetti from the rooftops! Deck the city with flags! Cover one another with flowers! Clap your hands and shout with joy, 'The revolution is here.'"

There was a practical down-to-earth reason for my joy as well. I found that by coming to this awareness I was able to reconcile a great number of things in such a way as to make it possible for me to love. No longer did I have to put so many things and people down. I had always rather blamed man for his past shortcomings. I had blamed organizations and governments for their narrow-minded actions of the past. I had blamed a great number of people and things in all kinds of ways. Now I was released from judging the whole past history of man, for I saw that all the people and all the institutions of every period represented whatever stage of evolution the world was in at the time. Perhaps if they existed today such institutions would be wrong and harmful, but they were the right ones for their time. I could no longer say that the religions, governments, and laws of the past were wrong; they had helped grow man into what he is today.

I perceived that whenever people tried to hang on to the old organizations and establishments past their time, they were misguided because they had actually evolved beyond them. When establishment's time has passed, it will strangle itself. Rather than resist or condemn establishment, it seemed more important to build new and better ones. I realized that new establishments could soon be built without the violence and subhuman means of the past, for soon people would have an awareness of themselves and the spiritual potential of their humanity which they hadn't had in the past.

I saw that the revolution will now accomplish what it hasn't in the past because people's arrival at this stage of being fully human marks the most significant moment in the whole evolutionary process. Stages of evolutionary process have been marked from the beginning of time

by the advent of different life forms. At each stage one
life form has been dominant on earth, more developed
and powerful than any other. After a time, a new form
emerges as master, and on and on up until the present.
For the past many thousand years subhuman paranoid
man has dominated the earth, but now we are at the
turning point. Man who still views himself as a distinctly
physical being, obsessed by fear—fear of hunger, fear
of attack by his own kind, fear of loneliness, and a host
of other fears—will no longer be in control.

Of course, fear-filled people as we know them will
not all disappear like the magician's rabbit. Probably
for the next century there will be people living by the
old limits of mind and nature, but they won't control
the world as they have until this age.

It seemed to me that the man whom evolution was
passing by was the fear-filled man gripped with paranoia.
What most people have called human nature has really
been paranoid nature. What they have called the first
law of human nature has actually been the first law of
paranoid nature. Any time anyone projects his fears outside of himself onto other persons, places, governments,
and things, and then lets those fears motivate him he is
operating out of paranoia. Any time anyone has a persecu-
tion complex which makes him believe that others are
out to harm him, any time he has a delusion of grandeur
which makes him feel he is mentally, physically, or spiritually superior to others, any time he acts out of sexual
frustration stemming from a doubt of his own virility,
he is operating out of paranoia.

I could see proof of the departure of paranoia in our young people. So many of the young I had come to know took paranoia or fear out in the open and looked right at it. They had an amazing ability to smell out dishonesty. They wouldn't brush it under the rug or let themselves be poisoned by it just because dishonesty was built into a system or was unintentional. The young refused to live with paranoia. They refused to put down natural man. They knew that fear and evil were not natural states of man but rather were his conditions when he was not acting out of his full humanity. The young demanded that life and man present wholeness. I saw then that the revolution to end paranoia was an actual end of life as we have known it. This was Armageddon.

I almost wanted to laugh when I wrote that. For so many years I had heard weird prophets trumpeting the end of the earth. Now all of a sudden I knew they were quite right. Perhaps the end wasn't the kind of end they envisioned, but it was just as dramatic and all-inclusive. I saw that our way of life was changing as drastically as it had when man came down out of the trees and began to civilize. With the disappearance of paranoia, all the nations, organizations, systems, practices, teachings, and forms which perpetuated selfishness and fear, which divided up wealth and separated man from man were in the first stage of becoming obsolete. When that day fully arrives, we will live as one big happy family. Hallelujah! It's here.

CHAPTER TWO

Off with Their Heads!

After I had arrived at my exalted conception of the ultimate revolution in 1969, I marched triumphantly into life, expecting to see the kingdom of heaven in full bloom. You can imagine what happened. Like Don Quixote, I charged full steam into solid walls which didn't seem to understand they were supposed to dissolve before my love. With my paranoia-free vision aimed ever upward, I tripped over so many personal problems that I didn't know whether I was standing up or lying down. I found that banquets of pie in the sky didn't fill my stomach. So I limped back to the drawing board for another look.

When I took another look, I found my basic ideas checked out all right, but I decided that I needed to discover some missing links in order for the chain of my conclusions to connect the old and the new. I felt that in my need to find continuity I wasn't alone. It seemed to me that a great number of those who had faith in the goals of the revolution were going about achieving them in the wrong way by being somehow tricked into resorting to the same methods that they said they wanted to do away with.

I usually try to solve a problem by getting back to the cause behind the cause behind the cause, so I started by looking at the surface injustices to which I was opposed. It was apparent that they were all brought on by human beings. Then I asked, "What causes a person to act out of their subhuman nature instead of their full capacity? In a world brimming with food, why don't people use their brains to get food to the right place at the right time? What makes people act with cruelty and lack of love for their brothers and sisters? Their instinct? No. They need to have a brain even to follow their instincts." Then I realized, "At the root of all of our troubles is the improper use of our thinking capacity, our minds."

Well, bless its little heart. I had been so aware and proud of my mind—that part of me which reasons, calculates, rationalizes, and collects knowledge—that I hadn't realized it had been busily churning away creating a mixed bag of blessings and mistakes. I had thanked it for its blessings but I had none-the-less gone out fighting other people, believing them responsible for errors that really lay at the doorstep of my own mind. I should have realized a long time before what a hassle my mind had given me. So many times I had seen the world as a dark and miserable place, only to view it as a rosy heaven the next minute. What had actually changed? Nothing except the interpretation my mind had put on things. At least, I realized that before I could point my finger at others, I should understand my own mind and get it pulled together.

I couldn't blame my poor mind though. Whenever I forgot my connection with life, when I lost sight of my true identity, when I lost my (God contact) then my mind was all I had left to run my life for me. The dear old thing rushed around doing the best it could, but it needed help from the rest of me. When I let my mind run things by itself, it was as though I was trying to operate a car on a third of its cylinders. I realized that in the Now Age man would live with his whole self—body, mind, and spirit. So if I was to live fully, I would have to understand how the mind worked and what its purpose was.

It seemed to me that my mind should be an instrument designed for my use, not vice versa. All too often it had run me as though I were its servant. It had kept me awake when it wished, it had made me heavy with gloom at times, and it had even made me hate. But obviously my mind was a necessary instrument for it had also helped me create, it had helped me translate awareness into action, to communicate, and it had even helped me experience God. Those teachings or religions which advocated hitting the mind over the head with a mental hammer or blotting it out by self-hypnotism missed the point. The mind is like a chisel in the hands of a sculptor. The sculptor needs a chisel to work with. He can't claw the stone with his fingernails. To become a master he must take good care of his chisel, keep it clean, sharp, and in good shape, but he has learned not to let the chisel run his life for him.

So in order to understand my mind I turned once more to evolution. It seemed to me that in the process of evolution, the development that separated man from the other animals was the evolvement of man's reasoning faculty. If there were some kind of chart indicating the different stages of development of life on earth since the first one cell amoeba, it would show a phase representing the advent of human existence. This phase would start with the evolution of the self-aware reasoning faculty and would end with the final full development and control of the mind. All in between would be the various stages of man's battle to gain control of his mind and to discipline it. Maybe that's what this revolution had really been about, the final control of the mind. After all, man's mind had now grown so strong it had created a scientific technology capable of turning the world into paradise— or of destroying it. The only thing that has stood in the way of our using the mind to create heaven has been the misuse of that same mind. When the misuse is finally eliminated, the human phase will be completed. That time is now, the Now Age.

At any rate, I couldn't blame the mind for not starting out fully developed or for starting out as such a mess. Right at its beginning, the mind was fed some inadequate information, and it had been acting on it ever since. Human beings evolved out of animal life, and wild animals live by the testament of the senses, so naturally the first information fed to our computerlike minds was information from the senses. Our minds took what they saw, touched, tasted, smelled, and heard to be the truth and acted on it. But the senses were highly inadequate authorities, and their information was far from accurate. Because the information was a lie, actions were based on fear. Fear fueled further fear, self-perpetuating misinformation, so human beings have never known what it is to be spiritually free, free of materiality, or haven't had the capacity until now. That is, except for a few who were our way-showers.

Many of the young, over this past twenty-odd years, have consciously or unconsciously wanted to erase the misinformation or limitations fed to them by the senses. That's why they tried to expand the senses. They have blasted the ears with sounds out of the normal hearing range, they have blasted the eyes with visually disturbing color vibrations, and some of them have blasted everything including their bodies with sense-exploding drugs. Many of the young also have the capacity to believe in invisibles, which free them from depending solely on sensual information.

When I saw what the kids were doing, I decided that the next time I charged out into the world I would have my own head in shape even if I had to take it off to work on it, not with drugs but rather with meditation.

This realization set off a chain of thoughts. Perhaps the French revolutionaries were not far wrong when they said, "Off with their heads!" The revolution seemed to be symbolized by a statement which was just as revealing: "Blow your mind!" That statement is still used today, and a great number of people have continued deliberately blowing their minds with drugs because, consciously or unconsciously, they have come to realize that their own minds are at the root of their problem. Many have become aware that their minds have been brainwashed with information hypnotizing them with false values, fear, and a sense of inequality so they have tried to use drugs to jar their minds loose. Others have trooped to psychiatrists, hoping to get their minds wrung out, and the greatest number of all have found the right way to do it, through meditation.

I remember at the time checking those ideas out by seeing how they fit with the two greatest heroes of the revolution, the first recognizably fully-developed and free men, Jesus and Buddha. I saw that they were really head-masters. They both told us to work on our heads. Both of them appeared to be advocating the overthrow of the governments and systems which would enslave mankind, but actually neither of them advocated the use of violence, neither of them advocated fighting the enemy on the outside of ourselves or resisting outside evils. They told us, "The enemy is our own mind when it is filled with judgment and fear."

Yet Jesus and Buddha were not impractical saints daintily walking around the country asking people to drop out. Their lives were no picnic. Buddha had to rip up all his roots, leave his family, and turn his back on money and power because of his realization that he had been duped by his mind into an illusory sense of self, and he left no stone unturned to find the way to freedom.

Jesus lamented, "The birds of the air have nests, the animals have holes, but the son of man (himself, the revolutionary) has no place to lay his HEAD." He even pinned it down by saying, "Take no (THOUGHT) for the morrow, what ye shall eat and what ye shall wear." Jesus really insulted the rational mind. Logic couldn't help but balk at his statement, "If somebody sues you for your coat give him also your cloak." It makes no rational sense. The mind would have to say: "You idiot, if you give away both your coat and your cloak, there's nothing to keep you warm. You'll freeze." Jesus wasn't logical.

So now I am back to the starting point of this reminiscence—how was I going to reconcile faith with the reasons for my human problems? Then I saw that my logical mind, which had tricked me into all kinds of self-defeating actions, had an Achilles' heel by which it was going to be put in its place without my having to fight it.

My logical mind had grown so strong that it was finally revealing its own limitations. It equated faith with perfection and absolutes, but there are no absolutes at the finite level. The mind said that I should abandon faith whenever I found imperfections in a thing or system, but now my mind had grown so sharp that it exposed flaws in everything—including itself. I saw that perfection at the material level was relative. If I made a million similar objects, a microscope would show me that no two are exactly alike, so which one would be the perfect one? None. Perfection is relative. I realized I would never find flawless perfection at the finite level, and that whenever I was tricked by logic into believing I could find any perfect person, place, or thing, I was bound to end in failure.

When I lost faith in law, I found faith in man. When I lost faith in man, I found faith in the source of that man, just as all of Jesus' disciples had to lose faith in him in order to find it in themselves. When I lost faith in my own self, I become free of the brainwashing which told me I was a limited finite man, and I found faith in God. When I lost faith in God, I found that I had faith in too narrow a concept of God. I found that the God I had faith in was a paranoid concept of God. I was using it as a weapon with which I hoped to overcome my enemies, as a policeman to keep life in line, as something apart from myself, off in heaven. When I lost faith in that God, I found God was really within me, *was* me.

Then what could I humanly do, I asked myself? A saying of Jesus' popped into my head: "Judge righteous judgment." I wasn't any longer to judge by appearances, no longer to judge in terms of a logical mind that puts things down by saying, "That's bad," or "That's good."

When I had looked out at the world through a lens colored by judgment, it was as though I was looking at a scene through a pair of cracked colored glasses. The scene was there. I could identify houses, trees, and people. But as long as I had the glasses on, those objects were all flattened out, the colors were gone, cracks ran through everything. However, when I took the glasses of judgment off, when I loved unconditionally enough to see without falling for good and evil, the world was there in all its glory. It was (and is) entirely different from the one I had seen through the glasses. Things had the same shape—I saw houses, trees, and people—but they were no longer distorted. Perhaps this is what the mystics meant when they said the world was illusion. The world seen through cracked colored glass is illusion.

Then I knew what Jesus meant when he said, "My kingdom is not of this world." He wasn't putting the earth down. The whole secret of his message is that the kingdom of heaven is right here at the material level if and when I can "see" it. He meant that his kingdom was not of the world dominated by subhuman nature. "This world" stood for the world of paranoia. He meant that when we put an end to paranoia his kingdom would appear right here on earth where it belongs, as it is beginning to.

I saw that the secret of untangling the confusion of life lay in understanding what the mystics call the third and fourth dimensions of life. They say that everything one can recognize at the phenomenal level, the world of effects, the everyday down-to-earth level of life, is the third dimension. Anything that can be named, labeled, or thought about is third-dimensional. The fourth dimension is the spiritual dimension, the total, the infinite where all is One. At the fourth dimension everything is comprehended in its pure being-ness, in its oneness and unity. The catch is that all thinking is limited to the third dimension. The fourth dimension, like God, is something that can be experienced but not thought about, for thought always limits. Thought divides. Spirit unites. The two levels are present simultaneously but not really understandable in terms of each other. Since

they are two different senses, one can't understand the
fourth dimension in terms of thought any more than a
blind man can comprehend color.

When Jesus talked about his kingdom he was referring
to the fourth dimension of life. In the Now Age people
will live in the fourth dimension as though they are
seeing without the colored glasses of judgment. As this
Now Age comes into full awareness we are both the
man of earth, operating out of our finite sense of self,
and the man of God, one with the whole of life.

My problem had been that I had gotten the two confused. A spiritual instinct sensed the reality of the fourth
dimension, but my mind tried to find it at the third
dimension. God existed at the fourth dimension, but I
kept looking to see God with my third-dimensional understanding. I kept trying to see God in war, in government, in establishment, but these things were part of
my man of earth self. I kept trying to bring God down
to this level, when the only way God could be experienced
was to take this level up to God by refusing to judge it
in terms of bad and good. Only then can Oneness be
experienced. When the fourth dimension is experienced,
a transition comes about. We are lifted to a higher vibration or sense of truth, and miraculously, when once more
we come down to the third dimension we find a kind
of healing or improvement has taken place. It's even
possible to become so in tune with this spirit dimension
that we can say as Paul did, "I live but not I"—though
he was operating at the third dimension, his fourth-dimensional sense of the allness was directing him.

That is what Jesus meant when he said, "I and my father are one, but my father is greater than I." He was saying: My third and fourth dimensions are one, but the fourth dimension is the greater. He wasn't talking about duality or separation. He wasn't going back to a belief in a God off somewhere. He meant that the inner man can manifest itself as the outer man.

It seems to me that the purpose of our revolution against subhuman nature has been to lead us into the fourth dimension, where we do not live by effects, where we do not "live by bread alone," or money, or guns, but where we live by virtue of our capacity to contact the infinite invisible, fully human, fourth dimension. The fourth-dimensional consciousness becomes ours, and our reliance, faith, and understanding operate out of the oneness of life, not out of our trying to find a power to use over our enemies.

The attainment of this fourth dimensional consciousness is what the mystics call illumination. It is the secret of harmonious living without strife, struggle, or paranoia. This freedom of illumination is really freedom from ignorance, for only ignorance holds us to the belief that life is dependent on things and people in the external sense. When we understand that our body, our mind, and our spirit belong to us and that we govern them, we become free. We are given a mind as a thinking apparatus so that we can think the thoughts we want to think as our man of earth self, but we can determine what we let occupy our mind. We are given a body, but we are not limited to that body except at the third dimension.

We are given a spirit to keep our minds and bodies pure. With these three we can lift ourselves into the fourth-dimensional consciousness where life begins to flow more by grace than by effort, where the I of us embraces infinity, and good can then flow forth from our consciousness into the visible.

The *Ultimate Revolution* is my exploration into ways of living which can help make the bridge from the third-dimensional world to the fourth, into the Now Age. It makes suggestions about how to work with both our earth-selves and our God-selves. It explores how we can achieve greater unity with our selves and others through our actions and our sexual instincts, how we can use the material effects of the world for greater wholeness and how we can contact the source of spirit for guidance. It is a journey from the darkness of the third dimension to the illumination of the fourth dimension. The Now Age is here.

CHAPTER THREE

The Morality of Grace

Have you ever watched a sunrise? When you sit through the long night, expecting a new day, some kind of faith is challenged when the clock says the sun is due to rise in three or four short minutes and there's still plenty of darkness outside, as though some sort of cosmic betrayal has taken place. Maybe your clock has gone crazy. Then, just in the nick of time, the light starts adding color to the world, the simplest objects begin to take on a sort of beauty and shriek out their right to be, that each of them has a purpose in life. You look at your own body, your own hands and feet, as though they are newly created wonders, and they too have a purpose. Everything has a purpose, and that mutual purpose welds you and all the world together into one being-ness.

That's the kind of position those of us who have been waiting through the dark revolution for the sunrise of humanity are in today. There is still a great deal of darkness around—in fact, it is sometimes darkest before the dawn—but the darkness has served its purpose. The world has slept. Now it is waking up and taking on its true colors. Who can help but be excited at the wonderful things that are happening now, full of light, no longer done in darkness? Everything has to be re-seen in the light of this incredible decade.

Most of us need a whole re-education as to "how" we should live in the light of day. We are so used to groping around on our hands and knees in the dark that we have to learn how to stand up straight in our full humanness, experiencing life rather than just touching it with our fingers. That's what this day, the one right at hand, is all about. The old world has been shook up by the revolution. The dust hasn't settled yet. There are pieces of the old ways lying all over the place that need homing—need to be mentally and spiritually lined up with their true purpose and place. It's time now for those of us who consider ourselves revolutionaries to start setting up guidelines for living in the light, or we will, as the old saying goes, win the war and lose the peace.

Perhaps we had better start by taking a look at ourselves. If everything has a place and a purpose—what's ours?

I personally have spent many years with a feeling that I was not in my right place and right time. I got along in the world, but I never felt quite at home. Now I realize that I *was* in my right place and in my right time, but the right time for the real purpose of my life just hadn't come yet. I'm a day person, a person of light. So are you or you wouldn't be reading this book.

Our real job isn't to tear down but to build up, and the day for building couldn't come until the revolution had finished tearing down the old or at least was nearing its end. At last it's the Now Age, and we can throw ourselves into life with the whole of our being, with the full sense of the rightness of the time and place— we are reconstructionists.

For that matter, I can see now that most of the people to whom I have felt drawn, of my close friends, are also reconstructionists. Some of them have worked for years, wrestling with metaphysical truths and stumping their toes on spiritual enigmas, always feeling that somewhere out there must be a world where they could feel more at home. Others have worked hard, been conscientious in their zeal to live up to the highest truth possible, only to see less qualified and less talented people achieve greater success in the world than they had. Most likely those of my friends whose success hasn't measured up to their industry and talent are in that dilemma because they are people being prepared for their place in the world of reconstruction. Their day just hasn't come yet.

Well, it's here now. It's the Now Age, and with it we can all see that everything in the past and everybody we met on the way was necessary for our growing into what we are today, and for our living of this day. If we felt confusion because our philosophy or religion has been unable to bring us the freedom that it promised, perhaps that was because just as we were being grown, so was our religion or philosophy being grown as well, growing from the dark into the light.

Apart from those of us who have been around for a long time, a whole generation of the young have been born who have been prepared from ages past for the job of being Now Age reconstructionists. The young of today leave no doubt that their differences are not simply modifications of past values; they are a whole new breed whose being is tuned to a different song. They sing the music of the new, paranoia-free world, the world where the sound of the mind has given way to the song of the spirit.

From my association with many of these young, I think it would be pretty safe to say there is little doubt that their instinctive and easy understanding of both the profound environmental concerns and the most mystical of truths qualifies them as children of light whose affinity for the reconstruction period isn't an accident. No wonder the young have been confused. They couldn't help but be concerned looking at the world of paranoia in which we have poisoned our atmosphere, let people starve, and talked love while shooting bullets. They had the capacity for love but were set down on the earth while the revolution was in full swing. They wanted to love everything and everybody, they wanted to be happy, but they were told that happiness was something to be worked toward for the future, not experienced in the present. They rightly couldn't understand why there had to be a disparity between what they felt and the way they were supposed to act. While we talked about the spirit, they felt it. They wanted to *be* it.

The young don't have to be sold on the Now Age;

they don't have to develop the sensitivities needed to live in it as do many of the older people; they don't have to "learn" how to love. They already "are." But they do need to understand what they feel, and they need to be able to articulate what they feel. For that matter, all of us who want to be part of the light world, who want to throw ourselves fully into growing tomorrow, into building the earth, need some "hows"—some guidelines. We are all in the same boat. We aren't young people, we aren't old people, we aren't black people or white people. Those classifications belong to the past; we are all one thing—reconstructionists, children of God.

We are all in the same boat for another reason: none of us can claim a nice pat set of rules on how to live in this new day. Each of us has something to contribute to the new way of life, but none of us has a complete answer. How could we? The new day has just dawned.

The world is on the verge of a new Now Age religion that will fit this new day, one that couldn't have evolved until the Now Age had actually evolved. Each one of us will add something unique to make up the wholeness of this new religion. As a matter of fact, the Now Age religion will be the creation of the collective consciousness, of total humankind rather than the expression of any one person. However, it will be like chemistry, where different ingredients are mixed together and end up making a totally new substance. A new religion suitable for the Now Age may be a curious blend of the old and the new, but it will be totally new.

We shouldn't be surprised that a new religion is arriving at this time. After all, the world has been here millions of years yet conscious awareness has become active only in the geologically recent past, and our discovery of the importance of consciousness has come only during the past century with the advent of psychology and psychiatry. Yes, we are on the brink of a totally new Now Age religion which will not only encompass the whole man but will also encompass total awareness of life at all levels, total experience, total space, total time—the total universe.

A New Morality

Speculations on a new religion might be good material for new day dreaming, but at this point we have a lot to do at a practical and much less lofty pinnacle. Today the emphasis has to be taken off the individual me *"I"* and be placed on the we *"I"* that we all share. All creations, even religions, will now be seen as a product of the universal Self of man. Paradox—that's not much different from what Jesus was trying to say, is it? So perhaps the totally new is totally old, but being new to mankind in general it is totally new. The important thing is that it is now.

At any rate, as an exploration into new territory, this book will be far from complete; it will just hint at a direction. I will be the voice for this particular expedition putting in my own two cents, but you are all contributing to it. If it adds up to some kind of "feel" for where we are going, if it can be reappraised and the routes retraveled until the waters of the Now Age are charted, it will have served a purpose.

We all know plenty of abstract truth. We have volumes

of metaphysical dissertation on the esoteric level of man's being, on his spiritual nature, on pure spiritual principle, and all of that can indeed be the source of our ideas. But if we don't get down to specifics, down to how to live as evolved human beings right now, it does no good. So let's look at some hows.

"How to live" implies a morality. It's hard to keep from shuddering at the word "morality." We associate it with the hypocritical morality of the past, but we still need some aids on how to live in this new decade, and that is what a morality is—guide lines to live by. When things are all going well, when we are in contact with our center, when we are in our right place knowing our true identity, nothing is needed; anyone who dares to grow, who dares to be creative, isn't always in contact. When we are out of contact we need some guidelines to keep us on the track until we find ourselves again.

The old morality was the morality of law, of the Old Testament. It was structured on the laws of bad and good, because it was designed for man who lived under the domination of his mind. He needed laws because he couldn't recognize his inner guidance. He didn't know the difference between his thoughts and his spirit. Because man couldn't realize in the dark that everything had its place and its use, he believed he had to protect his family so he made laws condemning everything which he thought was out of place, everything he didn't understand. He couldn't trust himself to find what things were and where they belonged in a way that wouldn't poison his spirit. Therefore, the old morality wasn't spiritual; it couldn't be. Laws are designed to resist evil, designed with a negative spirit behind them. All resistance is the result of fear, not love.

To put it another way, the old morality related to the third dimension, the level where man took the testimony of the senses and believed that life was limited to all the things he could identify with his mind, to the phenomenal level of life. At that level, self-preservation is paramount and everything falls under the title of bad or good. Everything has to be either one or the other.

A morality based on law inhibits freedom because law can't allow change. If the law is riddled with too many exceptions it ceases to be law. It has to apply to all people at all times, so law kills spontaneity in living. If we want to find a new morality, we must find one which offers guide lines for each situation while still allowing spontaneity in life. It is complicated because spontaneity requires change, and those afraid of change can't free themselves to follow it.

Now, the old morality of law was right for its time. It was indeed the best way to cope with the dark world, and it is still best for those who haven't developed spiritual sight. But that which was right in the dark is insanity in the light. Actually, this is pointed out in the New Testament. Jesus said, in effect: the purpose behind the law is fine but you can't fulfill the law at the level of the law, only by grace—or love. You see, love resists nothing, love has nothing to do with bad or good, love is never negative. Love is not only spiritual or fourth-dimensional, it is the very fourth dimension itself.

Then how about calling this new morality we are creating, our morality of love, the "morality of grace" to differentiate it from the old morality of law? Grace is a word signifying the action of love or the action of spirit. So, because a morality is nothing more than a collection of suggestions on how to act, a morality of grace is a list of suggestions or guidelines on how to live without violating the spirit of love. A morality of grace is only a collection of suggestions designed to aid those who know that they have no choice in the matter. They <u>have</u> to live fourth-dimensionally.

Then how do we start formulating this Morality of Grace? The first and cardinal test we can make for any action or thought is to see if the suggested action has any implication of bad or good. Whenever we put something down as being either bad or good, we are under the old law; we have accepted the belief in a power apart from God, the existence of evil, a world less than whole. You might suspect that there is no way to avoid this, but I don't agree. It can be done. We can find ways to be realistic and talk about moments of temporary light or dark without poisoning ourselves with condemnation or judgment.

For instance, we have accepted the fact that nothing has been created that's evil; only the use or rather the misuse of that thing is destructive. Everything is *for* some thing or some place. Because God created everything, everything has its purpose and place. We have no problem when things are in their right place, but we need a morality to help us face a thing which is not in its right place for doing what it is "for." So when we see painful or disturbing signs, our first job under a morality of grace, is to find out, or ask ourselves, "What's that for?" When we are faced with a person who troubles us, we can ask, "What's he for?" When we contemplate that which people and things are "for," we begin to see rightness in them. We are knowing the truth about them, and knowing is loving, so we are starting to love them.

As a matter of fact, we should always start with our own selves. Our number one responsibility is to keep ourselves in our own right place. So whenever there is a disturbance or personal frustration, we should start by asking ourselves: Am I in my right place? Am I doing what I am "for?"

Now this is not saying that we or everything else is at present in its right place, doing what it was created "for." Far from it. The light is just beginning to show us the truth. We have been knocking things over in the dark for so long that the world is a veritable jigsaw puzzle of misplaced people and ideas. It may take us many years to put ourselves as well as other persons and things into their right places, but this is how we can start.

When we see something that disturbs us, when we are tempted to return to the old judgments which trick us to say, "I'm bad," or "I'm good," we can stop. We can remind ourselves that it is all God, and then we can really look at the situation or thing and try to imagine how it could be, how it could belong, how it could serve a purpose. We can keep looking, keep refusing to judge until we find a possibly constructive purpose, because there is a purpose somewhere for everything. When we find it, we are free from condemning the situation. We can see that it appeared harmful or distasteful simply because it was out of place. The disturbance was a blessing because it was a signal telling us something was out of place so that we could set it straight.

After we have found out what something is "for," we will either see that it is already doing its thing and therefore we have nothing to fear, or we can help put it in its true place so that it can fulfill itself in a constructive way. When we help guide something back into being what it is "for," the destructive or inharmonious aspects will disappear. We call that a healing. This is done with no condemnation, no judgment, no resistance of evil, no trying to unsee or condemn something by claiming it doesn't exist—and incidentally, but most importantly, the disturbance is eliminated without our filling ourselves with the poison of self-condemnation or the poison we take on by condemning others. When we find what something is "for" without judging one way or the other we know what unconditional love is, both for our own selves and others.

It seems almost too simple to say that knowing what we are "for" is an act of self-love, but what could be more loving than to know we are united with God or being-ness? Rest assured, we are all where we should be at every moment when we realize that even our frustration came about to direct us toward fulfilling our reason "for" being in the world. Perhaps we can't always return either ourselves or others to their rightful place in the twinkling of an eye, but once we open our consciousness to try it, we are on the road. Don't forget, we are at the dawn of this Now Age and when the light is fully here, the universal house will be in perfect order.

Grokking and Grooving

Let's take this business of knowing what something is "for" another step. In the past we considered we "knew" something when we simply comprehended it intellectually and could call it by a name, but we were not living as total beings. When we began to experience the fourth-dimensional sense of life, we realized that "knowing" meant not only the report of the senses and the rational mind but also the actual experience of it as well. Knowing is not intellectual—it is a total involvement. In this sense, we don't know a work of art, a flower, a person, a mathematical formula, or any truth unless we not only understand it but to some extent experience and become it.

As long as someone thinks of himself as a separate entity cut off from all other people and life, he can't possibly experience things wholly. His nervous system can't take it, or rather, his feeling of security can't take it. As long as he thinks there is evil in the world, he can't allow himself to let go and freely experience life because of the fear that he might be crushed either by the evils from without or by the evils he finds within his own self.

Many people have to learn how to experience life. Reading about experiencing is one thing, but being free enough to open one's own self to it is another. The Now Age is an experiential age. Schools and seminars abound today for the sole purpose of teaching people how to experience life. When people begin to ache to experience themselves fully, ache to experience everything and everyone around them, it means they ache to experience God.

Perhaps the single most difficult element for the older generation to understand in its attempt to know the young is the importance the young already place on experiencing. If there is any generation gap, that is it. Older people have been conditioned in a world that was mental, rather than spiritual, in which the experience of a person, place, or thing was not consciously included as part of knowing. If they saw something and understood it with their minds, they thought they knew it, whatever it was. But the young have come along, more highly evolved, and they just naturally feel that to know something is to see it, feel it, touch it, think it, and experience it—if not "be" it.

Both the young and the old have been confused in their attempts to communicate with each other because when they have talked about "knowing" something they've thought they were talking about the same thing, but they weren't. The young thought the old people had experienced what they talked about, and the old couldn't understand that the young could not and would not really accept anything that they hadn't experienced. The old have been confused by some of the methods the young used, and the young couldn't understand why the old didn't appreciate their need to experience and to expand.

Many of the young have been lured into experimenting

with drugs in order to satisfy their need to "know" or experience life more fully because in the past there has been no existing morality which could help them do it in a natural way. The young have tried drugs hoping to feel new and different dimensions of life and not just extensions of the old ones.

A morality of grace helps us experience life more fully, and it fits both the young and the old. It will help the young to experience life as whole persons, in a natural way, and it will help everyone stretch until they can experience new dimensions of themselves and a life of total wonders. Since the fourth dimension must be experienced rather than thought, only a morality based on grace rather than law has the energy to lift us into the Presence.

In forming our new morality, it might help if we use some different words to help us, some experiential words. One I have always liked came from a book that was popular back in the "hippie" days. It came from the novel *Stranger in a Strange Land*, by Robert Heinlein, which has become a kind of classic. The word is a perfect experiential word, and I haven't found any other that quite fills the bill as it does. The word is "grok." It means a simultaneous combination of knowledge and experience.

To grok something means to understand it from all levels: to see it, to comprehend it, to understand it both spiritually and physically, to experience it, to identify with it, and above all, to discern what that something is "for." The hero of Heinlein's story groks people as well as situations. He often retreats inside himself until he can fully grok a situation or person. Then he acts, but his actions are not based on partial information, not on bad or good, for he has achieved not only the experience of the person or situation but also an awareness of the true multi-dimensional place and purpose of that person or situation in the overall scheme of things.

Another word from that period, which reached enough acceptance to be currently listed in Webster's Dictionary, is "groove" or "groovy." To groove on something means to zero in on it, to focus on it fully, to concentrate on it and put oneself fully into comprehending it. In order to grok something, it is necessary to groove on it.

We groove on a person, place, thing, or situation with our whole attention in hopes that we will arrive at the place where we can see if it is in its right place, doing whatever it is "for." Some of us old timers may smile remembering how popular the word "groovy" was in the hippie vernacular. "Groovy" was the adjective they used to describe successful grooving. When a person said, "Hey, that's groovy," he or she was saying that he or she had grokked the situation and saw how it fit in with the whole.

The word "groovy", like the more recent word "dig"— as in "I dig you, man"—didn't fall under the onus of being a degree word qualifying bad or good. Nothing is almost groovy. You don't almost dig something. It is either groovy or not, one either digs something or not; it either has been grokked and is groovy, or one hasn't grokked it yet and it isn't groovy. There aren't any set laws for what is groovy or isn't. What is groovy today may not be tomorrow, because tomorrow it may not be in its place doing what it is "for."

Actually, the importance of grooving on life is not all that new, but our realization of its importance is new. Jesus gave us explicit instructions on why it is necessary to groove on both where we are and the moment we are in. He said, "The ground on which you stand is holy ground." You should groove on it. No matter where you are, no matter where you find yourself, that very spot is holy ground if you really groove on it and grok it.

When we project ourselves into other places, when we spend time wishing we were somewhere else, we are denying that we are in our rightful place at that moment. Wanting to be somewhere else or in some other time is a put-down of where we are. Actually, if we really groove on the place where we are, really get the most out of it and understand it, we will be free to go elsewhere. If we are not where we think we would like to be, it is probably because we have not grokked or loved the place where we are at the present.

A cardinal suggestion we can add to our morality of grace is to be sure we are grooving on our present "here." We can examine it, see what it has to show us, look around ourselves, understand the holiness of the ground on which we are standing. We can bring our whole selves, body, mind, and spirit, and open our eyes to the grooviness of the spot we are in. Believe me, it will love us in return.

The next suggestion we can add to our morality is grooving on the "now." Jesus said, "Take no thought for the morrow. . . .Consider the lilies of the field. . ." and so on. How dare we waste the now and not appreciate it? We certainly will never have it again. At every moment we can ask ourselves: Am I fully grokking this very moment? Am I seeing it in all its fullness and richness? Am I cheating myself out of the appreciation of this very moment? Am I really experiencing this moment, or have I let my mind trick me into thinking about the past or future? Look at this moment. How many levels am I open to?

As long as we are looking over the shoulder of life, we are grooving on neither ourselves nor life. Of course, it is more pleasant to groove on the highs, but unless we learn to groove on the lows as well, we are not grooving on the moment.

In the past, we just wanted to escape from lows as soon as possible, to get rid of them, and that was all. Now we see that we must grok the lows. They have their purpose. So when we have a low, let's not be cheated. Let's experience it. Look at it. See what it has to tell us. Probably when we have grokked it, we will never have to experience that kind of low again. It will have served its purpose.

It's tempting to take a tranquilizer or drug in order to avoid lows, but by tranquilizing ourselves out of the lows we have denied a gift of life. If we have listened to what it is trying to tell us, tried to grok a low situation, tried to handle it with spirit, tried to lift it by reestablishing ourselves within and have been unable to make the difficult time pass, it probably means that the low is trying to tell us something we have refused to hear. If we cheat ourselves by taking a drug or drink, or any of the other outside dodges, such as sex-for-sex's sake, we may have simply pushed the low experience away from ourselves, and in the future we will have to go through the whole process all over again. We may have cheated ourselves of the lesson we could have learned. How much more fruitful and affirmative, how much more loving of ourselves and of our lives it would have been if we had grooved on the low until we had grokked it and found out what it held for us.

Up and Downs

Grooving on our lows is a lot like grooving on our mistakes. Often we try to ignore our mistakes or faults, but that's like trying to ignore a splinter. The sooner we groove on the splinter and see how to get rid of it, the sooner we are free of the pain or annoyance caused by the splinter.

Our mistakes are pretty much what the old morality referred to as sins. The old morality kept fighting sin and condemning it. When we didn't know to groove on sin, it grew into a monster. The only way to get rid of sin is to embrace it, throw it kisses, see what it has to say. Loving is knowing; when we understand the purpose of sin we love it to death.

The problem we have in understanding our sins or our mistakes is that they only exist at the third-dimensional level. The fact that they exist there must mean that they are necessary at that level. If we want a morality to help us arrive at the fourth dimension, we need to redefine sin so that it can be freed of the condemnation of the old morality.

Back in those beginning days, in order to avoid talking in terms of bad and good, you would hear the kids refer to *ups* and *downs*. Anything that lowers one into a darker sense of life was called a down, or *downer*, and anything that lifted them into the light was an up or upper. Downs make people lose contact with themselves. Anything that makes a person fall out of love with himself or herself is a down; it makes him or her fall out of love with God. You might say any down which alienates the self from God is a sin.

A great many acts we use to think were sins were not actually sins. They were sins only in that they managed to alienate us from our sense of God and self, but that was because we allowed them to make us feel guilty and bring us down. On the other hand, a great many things not considered sinful brought us down but we didn't recognize them as sins. For instance, nobody thought that pain, suffering, sickness, lack of love, too much play, too much work, too much food, too much or too little of anything, and all discomforts and frustrations were sins, but they separated us from wholeness, so that's what they were.

Do you get the point? This morality of grace has a way of looking at sin which takes the blame away from people, takes sin out of morality, and applies it to anything that causes people to feel separated from God. No one deliberately wants downs. They fall into them out of ignorance. If there is any blame, ignorance is the thing to blame. When we stop blaming ourselves, and see our sins as the collective ignorance we have fallen for, it is easier to groove on our mistakes and find out what they have to say.

Downs are like shadows; they exist on the way to the light. Once we are in the light, at the fourth dimension, we *are* the light and there are no more shadows. At the fourth dimension, there is no sin because there we are fully human. On the way we have shadows because they indicate the direction the light is coming from, the opposite of the shadow. They tell us something is blocking the light and they exist to inform us in which direction to head.

All of life is a matter of ebb and flow, of ups and downs. A perfect state of security, where there isn't any chance of downs, is really a state of stagnation. Nothing but slime grows in stagnation. If we want to be creative, we have to take a chance on downs. Even science tells us that nothing is created without tension, the pull of opposing forces. A ball won't roll on a flat surface unless it's being pushed. We have to see this in order to really know it's all God.

Downs and hardships are the fertilizer of life. They don't smell nice, in themselves they are not nice, but they do serve a purpose. They make us grow. If we want to be grown, we must learn to welcome them. Actually, we should be worried if we never have any downs or sins, for that would mean either we are fooling ourselves or we are not living creatively and pushing on to the fourth dimension.

Look at your own life. See how almost always your greatest heartbreaks, your greatest trials, your most profound setbacks have resulted in your greatest pushes forward.

We will not progress until we become grateful for our trails and tribulations. Our third-dimensional subhuman self is satisfied when it is at peace, tranquil, and secure with material good, but none of these feelings lead to real freedom. Spiritual freedom is above bad and good, sin or virtue. Our downs push us into wanting fourth-dimensional spiritual awareness, so even downs have their purpose.

Downs bring us another bonus. They make our ups more pure, more sweet, and more valuable.

While we are learning to groove on our downs and not put them down, we can add to our growing morality of grace by taking it another step: in the Now Age we shouldn't put *anything* down. Refusing to put anything down in no way implies that everything is allowed to run rampant, that there is no morality. There are hardships we all wish to eliminate, but we can do it without implying there is a power apart from God, by not blanketedly condemning anything.

Parents and the older generations who have learned lessons from the past can help others by sharing their experiences, but if they offer their advice in the form of a put-down, they show they haven't fully grokked.

Others, particularly the young, won't accept advice from those who have shown by put-downs that they haven't grokked. The young would rather pay the price of hardship in order to grok fully than to accept the shortcut of a put-down. Naturally, they would rather avoid a rough time if only someone could get the idea across to them in a way they could grok.

Another suggestion might be added to our morality. When it comes to our fellow men, let everyone off the hook. Whenever we hold another person under judgment, whenever we hold another person responsible, we have isolated him or her from the world. After we have found out what a person is "for," and after we have grokked the whole situation including our own place in it, we must let the other person off the hook. Most often we are not responsible for the other person anyway—we are not our brother's "keeper"—so it isn't our business to rush in and throw our weight around unless he has asked us to. If we turn him over to God and go about our own business, we have let him off the hook.

When it comes to someone with whom we are closely involved—a member of our family or an employee, for instance—once we have grokked the situation, we will find that the inharmony was caused by someone or something being out of place, not doing what it was "for." When we find what was out of place, we doubtlessly become aware of the ignorance or confusion that caused it, and then we can blame the situation but release the individuals from guilt. When we can let people off the hook, they can find themselves much more quickly.

Most important of all, we must let ourselves off the hook. When we have stumbled or fouled up somehow, we have to grok the situation in its full dimension using our minds, our bodies, and our spirits until we experience what it is all about. Then we must find in what way we were not doing what we were there "for," and finally release ourselves. As long as we have ourselves hung up, we are not part of the living whole, certainly not seeing ourselves as one with life.

An Appetite for Life

We are all stretching to infinity. That's the purpose of being. When the light of day is fully here, when the whole world has been Christed, we will all realize our infinity, but in the meantime we are stretching to it. We are all growing an appetite for life, and as this appetite grows, our ability to partake of more and more life grows. Now that we consciously realize the importance of grooving on the big and the little, on each moment, on each place, on each person and thing, we are taking a very big step toward being fully human. For many, particularly the older generation, this appetite for life is like a muscle which needs daily and conscious exercise in order to strengthen it and make it grow. Others, mainly the young who have been born with enormous appetites for life, need conscious direction and an awareness of the value of self-discipline.

Whatever makes us more living, more alive, more fully being, helps fulfill the purpose of why we are here. Anything that makes us less living, less fulfilling our life, is drawing us away from our purpose. So the golden rule of the new morality is: *Anything that makes me more living is an up, and anything that makes me less living is a down.*

Don't be deceived by the over-simple, untheological sound of that principle. It actually cuts right across our old morality. All of the things called "bad" by the old value system must now be reexamined to see if they can help make one more living, and the old "goods" have to be checked to see if they might possibly encourage stagnation.

Far more than just outlining a rule of thumb to live by, this golden rule really defines the difference between the spiritual life and the material sense of life.

People have made the spiritual life far too mysterious. It is really very simple. When I say "spiritual," I am not talking about lighting candles or spouting prayerful incantations to evoke some kind of magical intervention in the affairs of humankind. I'm talking about a plain old commonplace thing of which we can be aware at any moment we choose. At any moment, we can be aware of the spiritual and we can have recourse to spiritual power, because at any moment we can stop and realize what kind of spirit or "head" we are in, whether we are down, up, happy, sad, angry, negative, or positive. If we learn how to control our spirit, we gain control of our mind and our life and we are spiritual. It's that simple.

When we live in such a way that the spirit in which

we do things is more important than the result, we are living spiritually. Results are material, so when results are more important than the way we go about getting them, we are not living spiritually, but when spirit takes precedence over results, we are living spiritually.

It could be stated another way which underlines the revolutionary aspect of this new day. Jesus said we are always faced with two facets of life, and he gave us two commandments to follow: the love of God and the love of man, the invisible and the visible. But he said that the first and greater commandment is the love of God—truth, spirit, or the absolute. Until now the lesser, the love of the material, has been put first and the greater commandment has been second. Now we have a completely new day because the young and all of those who are revolutionaries are reversing the order. We will continue to have both sides, both the material and the spiritual, but in the Now Age the greater will be put in its rightful place and will take precedence over the lesser. Spirit will come before materiality or results.

The story in the Bible of Mary and Martha explains it another way. Martha worked, took thought, planned, and worried about material needs. When she got fed up with Mary's apparent lack of concern for household duties she complained to Jesus. He acknowledged the material need, but he let Martha know, "Mary hath chosen the better part." In the past our society was based on fulfilling the material or finite necessities first, but now the spiritual or absolute will take precedence, though both sides must be taken care of. Now the Mary in us will be more dominant than the Martha. Nothing new, just a reversal of importance.

The spiritual life is simple, but it's far from easy. It means that we can never let our spirit be one of resisting evil, no matter how justifiable the cause seems. It means that we can never condemn another person, no matter how evil he or she appears to be. It means that we can never let ourselves get depressed or down, no matter how we are persecuted. It means that we must never think down thoughts or perform down actions in order to get what we want. We must think first of the spirit, then of the results.

When Jesus told us in the Beatitudes, "Blessed are the meek," "Blessed are the pure in heart," and "Blessed are the peacemakers," he didn't mean that those qualities were good in themselves; he meant that persons who followed those examples were blessed because they were in the right spirit and their selves were not being poisoned by a bad head.

While we are on earth, we won't always be able to live spiritually, we won't have all highs, we won't reach a point where there are no "bummers," as the hippies used to call things that brought them down. We shouldn't want all highs and no bummers. When we have fulfilled our reason for being human and fully realized our oneness with infinity, we will be completely grown and will live *as* the high. Until then, we should be challenged by the hunt for a life with fewer and fewer downs and more and more highs.

When we have experienced the fullness of life—not

just bits and pieces of life, but life in its fullness, its richness, seen in every experience—we will truly express God. We will be loving life, and that means we will be loving God. We can say, "I know how to love God," because when we grok life we are living, and living is loving God.

CHAPTER FOUR

The Identity Dilemma

Life is a juggling act. While we were in the dark, we couldn't see life in its full perspective any more than a juggler can perform in the dark. In order to juggle, we touch only one ball at a time, but we have to keep our objectivity about all other balls at the same time, touching each one in turn. The ability to keep all the balls in the air is vitally important to those who want to live in the light of day.

When we pay too much attention to one aspect of life, our thinking becomes crystallized, frozen, hung up, up tight, a downer. In our morality of grace, if we let anything become crystallized into an abstract religious theorem, or if we become hung up on the material form and lose sight of its spiritual being, we are once more under the mind-controlled world.

At any moment we can stop and ask ourselves: Am I crystallizing this situation, or am I loose and free? If we are one-sided about anything, we can use our new-found guidelines to help us get free once more.

How do we know when we are free? When we don't

always have to take thought and are able to live by spirit, we are free. When God is living our life, it only means that we are living without having to think up answers, that our thoughts are not self-produced but come bubbling up out of our sense of freedom.

Almost every action we take is motivated out of our search for freedom—for God, if you will. Even the most down actions we perform are just misguided steps toward freedom. A man robs a bank because of the freedom he thinks the money will give him. As a child of God, he knows he is heir to all the heavenly riches, but he just goes about getting them the wrong way. A person commits suicide because he thinks his life is a prison and he wants out. People lean on drugs because they want freedom from the physical and mental limitations in which they feel crystallized. The desire all of these people have for freedom is an up, but the way they go about trying to get free may be the down.

Then how do we get free without resorting to downs? There isn't an easy way. We have to practice something which could, if we let it crystallize, become a down. That's why freedom is a paradox; we have to accept something which looks like the opposite of freedom in order to achieve freedom—that is, *discipline*, self-discipline. When discipline is forced, it becomes a down, but without discipline there can be no freedom.

Take, for instance, a ballet dancer, a football player, a scientist, or an astronaut. Such people have attained the freedom to perform the most intricate steps and maneuvers simply because they found discipline to be the key to real freedom. By disciplining themselves with daily exercise in order to build muscles, by learning all the techniques of their professions, they gained control and became free to do what they wanted. But discipline is tricky. If one becomes a slave to discipline, he isn't free to create on his own.

Most of us would like to do without discipline because it has been used as a hammer to hit us over the head, wielded by the old society which wanted us to conform or feel guilty. But we had better learn how to grok self-discipline in our morality.

When a person accepts a system of control, he is a disciple of that system, like being a disciple of a teacher. When a parent tries to discipline a child into conforming to rules and regulations, he is trying to make the child into a disciple of rules and regulations instead of freedom and self-expression. But when a person believes he will become free by fighting the rules, he becomes a disciple of anarchism and resistance.

If we want to be a disciple of our own whole self, we have to enter a discipline or training which includes three things: responsibility, commitment, and integrity (three words that reek of the old morality and must be redefined for use in our new morality.)

First, *responsibility*. Responsibility is a word made up of two words: *response* and *ability*. Responsibility is part of discipline because we do not have freedom unless we are able to respond and unless we do respond.

When older people complain about the young not being "responsible," they are really complaining because the young don't respond the way they *want* them to. Actually, many of the young are much more able to respond with their whole selves than the old are. By responding, the young are responsible. The old often mistakenly think they are being responsible just because they don't break any laws. Actually, many of them are not fulfilling their responsibility to themselves because they have become crystallized and don't know how to respond to life around them. They see the young struggling with a passion for freedom and criticize them, saying that the young are not responsible, whereas the very thing the young are trying to do is to live a life in which they do respond at all levels. Not until the mind-bound people, old or young, discipline themselves into being able to respond fully will they stop being irresponsible.

The discipline of being responsible has another side. Often the young dissipate their ability to respond by over-responding, thereby losing their balance. Sometimes they try to push their capacity to respond through the sound barrier and force it with such loudness, overstimulation, drugs, and the like that they dull their ability to respond on all levels.

A whole person is responsible because he responds to both his own reality and the reality of others; he responds to both material and spiritual needs. Yes, it takes the whole self to be responsible at all levels, but through discipline, a person can become an astronaut of the spirit.

Second, *commitment*. Commitment and devotion are the same thing. One is the action; the other is the spirit of the action. Everyone who is committed has accepted the discipline of putting his or her whole self into responding. They have committed or devoted their thoughts as well as their actions and spirit toward achieving the goal. Any who believe they can get what they want without committing themselves to it is trying to cheat. They are not taking their whole selves into it.

There are things we would like to have or do. We would like to be heroes, we would like to be respected by others, we would like to have a better world. We can have or do all those things and more, but let's not kid ourselves. We can't have or do anything without committing ourselves. But if we commit ourselves to doing nothing, we will end up having nothing and being nothing.

In order to achieve, we must devote ourselves to accomplishing what we want. Theologically, devotion is "the ready will to perform that which belongs to the service of God." Perhaps that is where the word "devout" comes from. Devout means committed. It seems like a contradiction, but we have to be devoutly committed in order to be free.

A ship not committed to a destination flounders in an aimless sea. A person who doesn't consciously commit himself or herself to personal responsibility to freedom wanders in the dark.

Third, *integrity*. In the past, a person's integrity was based on his ability to refrain from breaking man's laws. If that person was law-abiding, he or she thought they had integrity. Well, they did have mental integrity, but they didn't neccesarily have spiritual integrity.

Having a desire for freedom and the commitment to

it means little unless a person has the integrity to bring his whole self into life. Integrity of the body means keeping one's physical self healthy and ready to participate and using physical effort to achieve one's goal. Integrity of the mind means using the mind without letting it take over, without letting it fear or judge. Mental integrity also includes keeping the mind as a healthy instrument, so it can do its thing when it is called upon. Spiritual integrity means the capacity to keep an "up" head, always remembering that the spirit of an action is more important than the result.

For instance, there are times when we are committed to a job or to an act of creating, perhaps even to helping or healing another person. If we have lost sight of our commitment—have allowed ourselves to become confused or dulled by outdated concepts, too much drink, negative thoughts, or some drug, and have become clogged up with a lot of down vibrations—we will be of no use to anyone at those times when we are suddenly called upon for help. Here again is a form of discipline. We must have the integrity to ask ourselves if we are being devout toward our commitment, if we are being responsible, if the freedom we are after isn't more valuable than whatever we are doing that is keeping us from living it. We must choose what we want most.

The hardest and most important part of integrity is having the honesty to be ourselves at all times. A person who refuses to put on a face of commitment without being really committed has integrity. A person who refuses to follow laws that he doesn't feel right about in his heart has integrity. A person who is not afraid to stumble and fall if that is where he is at has integrity. A person who is not afraid to respond honestly, even though he may be looked down upon by others, has integrity. A person who takes on commitments without fearing an inability to fulfill them shows the integrity of self-love.

Making mistakes does not mean a lack of integrity, but when a person tries to act as though he is something other than his own state of consciousness, tries to pose as something he is not, shows by his falseness that he doesn't have integrity. A person who lives up to whatever degree of truth he or she has found has integrity, while someone else who actually knows much more but doesn't quite try to live up to what they know has little integrity. They are not true to themselves.

That is why the last and the most difficult price we pay for freedom is the discipline of knowing our own selves. Unless we know who we are, we can't possibly have the integrity to respond honestly and commit ourselves fully.

Knowing Ourselves

Nine times out of ten, we have lost our freedom and integrity because we have lost our sense of who we are— or we have never known who we really are. When we feel a loss of freedom, we usually try to blame a particular problem or some person who has hung us up, but it may be something simple and ordinary which has tricked us into a false picture of ourselves, something as simple and ordinary as a label.

A short time ago a friend invited me to her house

for a Saturday afternoon party. As each of the thirty some odd guests arrived, the hostess announced a few simple rules for the afternoon. She explained that she had deliberately invited people who did not know each other, people who were all experts in their fields, and that she did not want us to tell our last names to each other or to divulge our professions. We were otherwise free to talk about anything we wanted to. Well, you never saw such a helpless group. There we were, a room full of successful people who didn't know how to talk to each other without the identifying labels of doctor, lawyer, merchant, or chief.

The result of the game was that everyone listened to everything everyone else said, no one judged, everyone treated everyone else with respect, everyone was warm and fraternal, no one was superior. The room was full of people, not labels.

If you think you know yourself, ask yourself: Who am I? See how far you get without labels. I did, and I was shocked to see how I had let labels isolate me from the whole world. First I said I was a male, and that cut me off from half of the other human beings because half of the world's population is female. Then I said I was a white male, and I cut myself off from all my black, yellow, and other brothers who are not white. In fact, I cut myself off from all but a fraction of the world's population, because by far the largest percentage of the world is not white male. Then when I added, "I am an American," the noose got even smaller. When I accepted labels for city, religion, age, and so on, I finally isolated myself from the whole world.

Acceptance of labels might seem innocent and harmless except for the fact that once we have accepted them for ourselves, we start living by the laws of those labels, within the confines of those labels, and we are no longer free. The minute we label ourselves anything, be it man or woman, liberal or reactionary, establishment or hippie, old or young, we are cutting ourselves off from pure being-ness.

The desire not to be a label has motivated most of the rebellion of the past. Many have rebelled against accepting a professional label which would trap them for life into a single type of job. Many have rebelled against being forced into patterns of life which would routinize them and eliminate spontaneity in life. And many have rebelled against having to live under the label of an ethnic group or class.

Apart from those who have rebelled, many have become aware of wanting to be free of labels by studying books on the importance of one's self-image and how to change it. It is perhaps a good thing to improve our self-image, but ultimately one label is just as bad as another, and we aren't really free until we have gone beyond labels altogether.

Truly knowing oneself is like knowing God—if you have a name for it, it isn't. That is why man has been so often defeated in his quest to know who he is. He can experience himself, but he is constantly changing; in order to know who he is, he has to keep experiencing his own consciousness over and over. His name means nothing unless he knows what state of consciousness his name represents at the precise moment he is using it.

Basically, the mystics are right when they tell us we are spirit rather than body. If any one aspect of the whole man has to be considered more important than the others, we will have to say that it is man's spirit self. At best, we are that which is making the body function, making it live, the very life within the body. We are not so much the physical body as that which is happening in and through the body. If we really want to know ourselves fully, we must know that we are what we see with our eyes as well as what we recognize with our minds, and at the same time we must know we are really consciousness which manifests itself as body, mind, and spirit. Our job in life is to be infinite enough to be able to know all aspects of ourselves at once without isolating any single side as though it were the whole of us.

Our goal is to see God as everything including ourselves, but as human beings, we cannot exist in the world without assuming some identity. The problem is that when we have too much personal identity, it turns into egotism and cuts us off from our source. On the other hand, mental institutions are full of people so wrapped up in a sense of the infinite impersonal that they can't identify with self and they have ceased to function at this level. In India, some have even experienced a kind of samadi—ecstasy—in which they lose their sense of identity to such an extent that they die.

Jesus knew he had no being apart from God's, yet he answered to his name; he said "I" referring to his personal identity, even his body. So what do we do?

How do we cope with this dilemma of being both a personal man and an impersonal God?

In this new day, we don't put anything down, we cope with this dilemma by realizing that being alive is a fluid state. To understand this takes grokking, to insure against crystallizing anything into one-sidedness. Our lives are living, which means that they are constantly on the move, and so is our own sense of identity. At every moment, we are either putting on a covering of personal sense or we are stripping off layers of personal sense. We are never stuck in a perfect state of dead balance between the two.

The best way for me to explain how this operates is to show how it works for me. Every time I get involved in some sizable public activity, such as producing a play, publishing a book, or being involved in any public creative venture to which my name is attached, I go into it with the knowledge that I might have to pay a price. I can't avoid involvement by feeling I don't want to pay a price, otherwise I wouldn't be living up to my personal integrity by experiencing what life has for me. So I plunge in.

Each time I get more and more caught up in a whirl of personal contacts, public appearances, television, radio, and speaking engagements. Bit by bit, a sense of a personal self grows deeper and deeper. I become more and more aware of myself in relation to other people, in duties to perform, in time schedules where a "me" has to be a certain place at a certain hour. By the time my duties are completed, I am well aware of a me who now fits a number of labels. It becomes increasingly difficult to get silent within and feel God. I get over-aware of myself as a body and mind and a feeling for my spirit self slips away. Having learned the hard way, when I start a project I now know not to make commitments any further along than necessary, so as to have time for a retreat on completion of the project. When my activity is over, the pendulum begins to swing in the other direction. My sense of personal self begins to be scrubbed off of me. Naturally, my identity isn't happy with the scrubbing. I go through hell. It's no fun, but having too much personal sense becomes a down and the down causes the purging. After a matter of weeks, sometimes dark weeks during which I have to make myself remember to groove, I once more stand naked, or emptied of identity.

Once more, there returns the feeling of my being lived by a deeper sense of myself than my human identity, and with it all, the glorious sense of freedom that comes from releasing the world of judgment and separateness. I no longer feel I am a businessman, author, lecturer, or any of the other labels. I am just me—one with God. My moments in meditation become powerful and clear once more.

Then it starts all over again. When I am recharged and transparent, I am once more ready to share. Everything is so groovy I start getting involved again, even though I know what it means to take on self-awareness. That's as it should be, because as long as I am on earth

I want to be fully alive. I am always either putting on personal sense, which means I will sooner or later have to pay the price of being purged, or I am already in the process of suffering the ego loss that I need in order to once more be free and creative.

This example is an oversimplification. However, it applies not only to human identity but to all forms of our creative and spiritual life. Each of us must assume a personal identity in order to work in the world or create. While we work, the awareness of transcendental being-ness decreases in ratio as the personal sense increases. The whole process is not a matter of bad and good; it is a creative tension which keeps us from ambivalence, keeps us from dropping out of the world by not being all we should—both man and God at once.

Man of Earth

In order to have the integrity to know ourselves at any given moment, we have to understand both major views of self—our personal man of earth self and our spiritual man of God self. Unless we understand and love both of these aspects of self in their fullness, it is impossible for us to know where we are as the pendulum of our consciousness swings from one awareness to the other.

Ordinarily, when we talk about the whole man, we are referring to the man of earth in his wholeness, which is rather like referring to the Trinity in its three aspects. The Trinity makes up one whole, but humanly we see it as three parts. The closest we can come to knowing anything or any activity on the finite level is to see it in terms of a trinity of physical body, human mind, and divine spirit.

There are three kinds of man of earth, for that matter. Look at the people you know. You will see that each fits one of these three. One person is more body-conscious than anything else. He primarily responds physically, and secondarily mentally or spiritually. Another person primarily responds in terms of his mental self, with the physical or spiritual following in importance. Still another responds with spirit first, body and mind afterward. Everyone has all three aspects, but one aspect is always more dominant than the others.

In order to know our man of earth selves, we have to know the extremes of each of the three aspects of ourselves, almost as though we were seeing ourselves as three different people. When each extreme is understood separately and in depth, it can be reconciled into a whole. Then we can recognize when any aspect has atrophied or overpowered the other aspects.

Body man not only has a physical form which needs to be understood and kept in good shape, but he only responds physically to the things he encounters. Like responds to like. Abstract or mental theorems don't register with the purely physical person. All that person's responses are physical and come only from physical identification with other persons or things.

A body person can't identify unless he has another body to identify with. In order to learn, he needs a guru or teacher to learn from or to whom he can relate his actions. That is why primitive people and the class of people who are involved with the more physical aspects of life have to have a personal savior to identify with.

There is no need to put down those who want a physical teacher or avatar. As each one of us includes a physical man, though that side may not be predominant, we all need at some time in our lives, a personal savior with whom to identify. Perhaps we are guided mentally or spiritually more than we are physically and feel we don't have to look up to any human being. If so, we may be ignoring the purely physical side of our natures. We will find ourselves operating more wholly if we begin to include a personal ideal. Those of us who shun becoming disciples of a Jesus, Buddha, or even some modern teacher are cheating ourselves out of wholeness. We will never find the God of ourselves until we have witnessed it in someone else. Self-consciousness about deifying another person is the mind's attempt to keep us under its control. We had better get simple and let ourselves personally love a Jesus or a Buddha to be balanced. We may not often have to identify at that level, but at times it is necessary. Accepting a personal teacher with personal identity may be considered the lower corner of the trinity, but it is in no way inferior or less important than the other aspects. Anyone who believes that a physical response to anything is inferior to the mental and spiritual responses is equally wrong. When we eliminate our awareness of the need to respond physically, we are out of balance and it might be good for us to deliberately find ways to do so. Sometimes a physical pilgrimage brings the physical aspect of ourselves into line. In a simple way, lighting a candle, or saying a personal prayer, may do it. At any rate, not to expect the physical side of man to respond physically or emotionally is a condemnation of part of one's own self. Far too many intellectuals and far too many metaphysical students have been tricked into this rejection of their whole selves.

The next part of our whole selves is the mind. Mind man goes wherever he lets his mind go. Anyone who thinks he can be whole by using his body and spirit without bringing his mind into the trip is doomed to wobble on an unsure course. Perhaps physical man is doing his thing by building his churches, participating in rituals, and offering his tithes, but unless his mental side is making every effort to understand the meaning behind it all, he is tangled up in blind faith, and faith that is not balanced with logic is just that—blind, unseeing.

Now, as body man needs a teacher with whom to identify, mind man needs teaching. Teachings are mental, and naturally the mind identifies with them. To "know thyself" is the highest form of mental expression; to know the absolute self is to know God. So the more absolute the teaching the mind can comprehend, the better.

If mind person hasn't found a teaching he or she thinks is right for them, they must keep looking. The fact that a person continues to use the mind to investigate keeps them whole.

Mind person doesn't have to focus on a Jesus or Buddha, a human identity, but he or she has to recognize that it is possible to have a Christ or Buddha consciousness within themselves. He or she has to be able to see that there was a Jesus, or a Moses, or a Mohammed who had the Christ consciousness. The Christ consciousness is present whenever a person has seen himself or herself as one with God—no matter what name it is called by. It is necessary for the mind to accept that this has happened to others so that it too can eventually experience God.

Mind person must also have the integrity, as I said earlier, to keep the mind trained, educated, and not too drugged or cluttered with useless value judgments so that it is ready and able to be called upon when the mind side is needed.

The third aspect of our whole selves is the spirit self. Within each of us is the capacity to make contact with the truth of our being, to feel it and experience it beyond the purely mental and physical. Within each person is a deep well of peace, or the possibility of resting in a real and recognizable feeling of universal oneness. It's a kind of joy. Joy isn't physical and it isn't emotional; it's a kind of exaltation. If we are not able to experience this peace and joy, we are not whole, not even whole men of earth.

That's why laughter is so important. Heavy, dreary "religious" people who walk around in gloom, never laughing, are ignoring their spirit selves; there is no joy. Instead of saying, "Families who pray together stay together," I would like to say, "Families who laugh together love together." There is nothing more beautiful in the world than a family of old and young who are all laughing together. It shows they are a whole family—physically there, mentally free, and spiritually full of joy.

Whereas body man needs a religion with a personality at the forefront, and mind man needs a religion with high ideals, spirit man needs the capacity for love or mysticism. Any teaching, religion, or philosophy has to include the possibility of the actual experience of God to be whole. Any teaching that helps its people attain this inner contact is spiritual. A teaching may be mental and it may be physical, but it isn't spiritual if it ignores the need for us to have the mystical experience ourselves.

Of the three sides, the spirit is usually the last to develop and is the one most needed today in "wholing" up mankind. The advent of our capacity for the third side is what marks the end of the dark period. Because spirit is light, in the mental-physical day there couldn't be a sense of universal light. That's what the revolution was about—freeing us from the mind and body domination so that all three sides of us could make up a whole. The three parts and their manifestation form a kind of triangle within a triangle: body self needs to see a Jesus as God, mind self needs to see itself as God, and spirit self needs to experience God.

I have used religion as an example, but a whole man responds in all his activities with the full trinity of self. If any job or relationship has broken down, we can examine the situation to see if one of our selves is not functioning properly.

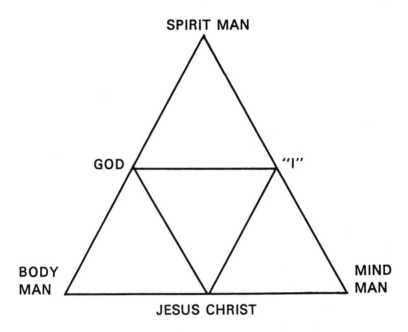

For instance, often a person who considers himself or herself a spiritual student will conscientiously study and pray, but then they become confused because they haven't manifested supply—no money. They will have an abundance of spiritual feelings but few of the earthly or material things they want. This is probably because they aren't responding with their whole selves. Our getting comes from our giving. If we want material things, we have to give of our material selves. We may not receive back from the same place where we gave, but we will receive if we give. Even if we have only a few drops of oil, as the Bible story goes, we must begin to pour. We can begin to pour by something as small as giving a stick of bubble gum to a child or offering a flower to some down person who needs it.

We should also contribute at all levels of self to any teacher, teaching, or activity from which we want to receive. We must contribute from our possessions, our mind, and our spirit. We are simply not going to receive from anything we don't give to.

The same applies to our jobs. A lot of people complain that their work is a drudgery. They are probably offering the job their minds and bodies but not their spirit and love. No matter how mundane a job seems, if we offer it our whole selves, if we honor and love it by taking our fullness into it, the job will honor us back with joy.

Actually, we respond wholly for a very selfish reason. There isn't any God up in heaven keeping score. The simple truth of life is that if we want to receive, we create our own receiving by giving. In direct mathematical ratio, the more we give, the more we get. We can receive from a teacher, job, or loved one for a while without giving from every level of our self, but before long we shouldn't be surprised if something takes that person or activity out of our lives or if the relationship seems to dry up. Wholeness wasn't there. We would be wrong to think it has happened by mistake or accident; consciousness was at the root.

The Man of God

No one has ever seen the man of God. He isn't in this world of recognizable being. No one has ever seen you. No one has ever seen me. I have seen bodies, I have recognized personalities, but I have never seen the truth of those people. If you think you have seen me you are mistaken. I am even mistaken if *I* think that I have seen me. I may have looked in the mirror or seen a form in a photograph, but that wasn't me. Sure, I have had bodies, maybe many of them, but you or I have never seen me by seeing my bodies.

To begin with, I had a tiny eight-pound body when I was born to this name with which people try to identify me. But that body was entirely different from the one they identified me with a few years later, and there certainly is little resemblance to the one I am associated with now.

As for that, reincarnation, the belief that one has many lives, is probably the best known way of explaining that I have been here since the beginning of time and will be here until all eternity. If you guessed at some of my past lives, or if you thought I was only this present one, you would be wrong. I can't be known with any faculty you possess. You can experience me, fourth-dimensionally, but you can't know me by any method which differentiates.

Neither am I limited to any nation or place, not even to any planet or universe. I am limited only by the limits of the kingdom of God. I am not limited to being a man. I am not limited to being a woman.

I am perfect, and so are you; I have always been perfect. I have never made a mistake. I have never lacked love. I have never been anything but immortal, God-created,

God-maintained, and God-fulfilled, and neither have you. . .

Certainly this kind of talk offends the mind. The mind just can't grasp it. You could well ask, "How can a grown-up man say that he has never made a mistake and never even been seen?" And to anything which speaks as a you or a me, those statements can't be understood. But, as I said before, a human identity with its body, mind and spirit exists at the third dimension, and at the fourth we are our completely naked, self-purged, identityless selves. This fourth-dimensional self lives in silence. It stands face to face with itself only when all words have stopped, all multiplicity is gone, in a state of unconditioned being where all is God. This self is the one which never makes mistakes and is never seen. Surprisingly enough, this state can be experienced.

Perhaps another statement of Jesus will illustrate. He said, "I am the vine, you are the branches, and my father is the husbandman." And, "If you abide in me, you will bear fruit richly, but if you are cut off, you will wither and die. " Well, just point out the window at a vine. What is your finger actually pointing at? It isn't pointing at the vine; it is pointing at a part of the vine. Nonetheless you say, "There is a vine." You can't point at all of the vine at one time, can you? Though your finger is pointing at one of the vine's branches, it is pointing at the vine.

But within that branch is all the life of the vine, all the qualities of the vine, so that the branch is fully one with the vine. It derives all its good from the vine, which it really is at the same time that it is a single branch. From one side, we could say that we see the vine when we see the branch, in much the same way we say we see a person when we see a body, but both would not quite be true unless we included all the branches of the vine and all the leaves, roots, etc.

In life, that is impossible because infinity is too large to identify, yet you are actually one with that total infinity, so you would have to say you saw infinity before you could say you saw me or anyone else.

Here is how that works: perhaps there was one seed to begin with. It grew into a vine, and that vine bore thousands and thousands of grapes full of seeds. Many of these seeds fell onto the ground or were carried by birds to other lands. Each time the seeds began to grow, they became vines themselves and in turn produced more seeds and on and on and on. Yet the only life was really a continuation of the spark of life that was in the first seed, not separate lives but the expansion of that one life. So even when you point at or try to identify a whole vine, you are cutting it off from its true self, which is really all the other vines as well.

When we feel we have a life apart from that Christ spirit, we have cut ourselves off from the vine, and when the vine doesn't recognize the husbandmanship of all of life, it becomes cut off.

In another way, though each individual is much more than its individual manifestation, it is still complete within itself. Each grape on a vine is complete in its form and needs nothing from any other grape. Yet each grape finds its completeness from the invisible source to which every grape is connected. Because it is connected. Because it is connected to the source, each grape is every other grape, though it is complete in itself.

To humans, or to all beings for that matter, the source of each person is the light, which is God. Each person has a light body which gives rise to the visible body, but the light body itself is invisible. It is the truth of the person, the other end of the wholeness.

When we hear that the search for the self must be conducted within, no amount of mental or physical surgery can help us find it in our body. The part of us for which we must look within is the *I* at the very center of our being. And when we find it, we realize that our spiritual integrity is our ability to turn to that *I* within for all our guidance, our inspiration, our fulfillment. We must realize that this *I* within us needs no man, for this *I* is not dependent on "man whose breath is in his nostrils."

This *I* doesn't have to announce itself. This *I* is an invisible presence that is always with us. At any moment, this *I* is there for us to turn to, inwardly and silently.

Stop. . . right here. Now, forget everything I have just said. Feel what I was trying to say. Feel a presence which is within you. That is the *I* that was being talked about.

To get a feel of that *I* is to enter the fourth dimension. Third-dimensional man is indeed body, mind, and spirit, and we must know and relate to all of those aspects because we do operate in the third dimension much of the time; but actually we are always both dimensions at once. Our ability to comprehend from the fourth dimension is growing greater and greater and will continue to grow until the glorious day when we live fully fourth-dimensional lives.

This fourth-dimensional I is not earthbound. It has no limitations. It is the unconditioned self. It is the real spirit self, the universal self.

To think of unconditioned self is one thing, but to experience it is another. That is what makes it fourth-dimensional, because the fourth dimension can only be *experienced*. When we surrender our limited view of ourselves, when we let go of believing we are seeable and knowable, we are loving ourselves fully. When we stop trying to believe we know others, when we see their third-dimensional expressions, we are loving them, we are healing them, and we are praying for them.

The spiritual life is the recognition of the unseeable spirit *I* within. This spiritual life recognizes that the *I* of you and the *I* of me are the same, and if I am and you are, God is. Therefore the recognition of I AM-ness is the way of love, the life of love, the substance of love. And the secret of mysticism. Now I know what self-respect is. When I have identified with the life source within, I have true respect for myself. When I see with my *I* and not my *eyes*, I know who I AM.

CHAPTER FIVE

The Necessity of Others

The first time I heard oriental music it all sounded alike to me. I was so used to the limitations of the eight-note scale that the freedom and variety of limitless sound turned into one big blur. But when I began to hear and understand the subtle, rather four-dimensional quality of Hindu music, I got more and more fascinated by its exquisite variety.

The same confusion came over me when I first glimpsed the limitless vistas of understanding that opened up when I was able to understand both my third-dimensional self and my fourth-dimensional self. I began to see and understand things I never knew were there before. My ability to enjoy life and to love others became potentially infinite.

At the fourth dimension, we are inseparable from all others, so it isn't a matter of loving or not loving—all just IS. But in order to reach that lofty and delightful state, we have to start by first understanding how to love others at the third dimension.

In order to love anyone else, it is absolutely imperative

that we start by loving ourselves. That is why I have so often said that our first responsibility is to our own selves, that every action is rightly a selfish one.

Selfishness is no longer such a down idea when we realize who we actually are, that we are one with all others, just as a branch is one with the vine. But for the same reason, what we do with ourselves involves our duty to all humankind. We must think of ourselves first because when we let ourselves get down, in a small way we are dragging the whole of mankind down with us because we are all hooked together. When we lift ourselves up, we are lifting all of humankind. Jesus said, "I, if I be lifted up, will draw all mankind unto me," because he realized he was connected with all mankind in the one body of humanity. He could just as well have said "I, if I fall down, will drag all mankind down with me."

Here is where double-thinking comes in. On the one hand, I must think primarily of myself, for I will be no good to anyone or anything if I am not healthy and alive at all levels of my being. But on the other hand, I must realize that all mankind has to be lifted so that I, by being one with it, will rise with it. I can't just say, "To hell with the world. I will lift myself no matter what happens to everyone else." Perhaps my consciousness, my head, is high most of the time, but I am tied to humanity and I personally won't get much higher until all of humankind rises higher. If I want to stay high, the whole human family has to stay high.

Before long it will seem incomprehensible that in the

past we had to teach people to treat others with love and respect. When the light has fully come into our collective consciousness, we will realize that our conduct toward others has nothing to do with the old morality of right and wrong, of having to make oneself be a good instead of a bad person. We will realize without a shadow of a doubt that we are joined to all others in one self, much in the same way as we are joined to our own hands and feet. Everyone knows that an infected finger affects the whole body. Only our third-dimensional sense of self, which accepts the illusion of time and space, tricks us into believing that we are not joined with all others.

Anyone who has caught a fourth-dimensional sense of self for one split moment knows that to commit violence on another person is like whacking one's own fingers with a hammer or sticking pins into oneself—mental, physical, and spiritual insanity. Being considerate of others isn't good; it's just plain smart and necessary. Absolutely everything we do to any other human being we are doing to ourselves.

That's why forgiveness and gratitude are so vitally important in the morality of grace. Forgiving another person has nothing whatsoever to do with being good or noble. It is a purely selfish act, and a purely necessary one. Whenever we hold any animosity toward another person, we are not loving our own selves. In direct ratio that we feel hate or disgust toward another, we are swallowing a kind of spirit poison because we are bringing our own selves down. When Jesus said, "If you have aught against your bother, go and forgive him before you come to the altar," he couldn't have spoken more simply. We go to the altar to love ourselves; that is a pure impossibility so long as we hate ourselves through hating another.

Gratitude works the same way as forgiveness. Whenever we are grateful to another person, we imply that something or someone besides our own finite selves can bring good into our lives. Our gratitude kills our separateness because it recognizes that we are not alone and cut off, not complete within our finite concept of self. Gratitude actually shows that we know who we are. When we show gratitude to others we are showing it to life or to God expressed *as* the other person. Gratitude is the recognition of the divinity within others and within our own self.

As silly as it sounds, there really aren't any people in the world. There are states and stages of consciousness expressing themselves in many different forms, but there is only one self. When we are really aware of that, we see ourselves in all people and would no more think of trying to lie, cheat, fool, or trick another person than we would deliberately try to fool ourselves.

When we realize this oneness, we will automatically know that in life we must contribute to the oneness as well as take from it. Like a community bank account, if too many people take and not enough give, the community of humankind goes bankrupt. In fact, that is what was happened to bring the revolution about. We knew we had to jar the mind out of leading us into spiritual bankruptcy, selfishness.

The Mystical Marriage

In order to contribute my part to the universal bank account I have to understand my relations with other people. I have to know both how my Man of God self relates to others and how my man of earth self relates. The man of God is the real truth of myself and a consciousness I will grow into, but by far the greatest time is taken up at the level of my Man of Earth self and its problems. However, without some sense of my absolute God self, I can't design a morality to help my earth self in relation to others.

The whole purpose of the monastic life, advocated by the mystics, has been to lead people into a state in which they experience a total absorption in God, their mystical selves. In order to achieve this state, it has been believed that a person should cut himself off from all human contacts, that a potential mystic should eliminate all human emotion. It has been taught that while a person was in the world of family and business, it was impossible to become unattached; one should therefore retreat from society and forcibly, if necessary, eliminate any emotional attachment to other people.

When one is locked up in a monastery, the theory implies, the personal sense of self becomes so lonely, so desperate, that it finally lets go and finds its allness in a God sense or God awareness. After having found that, the monk or nun sees God in everything and everyone and never feels lonely again. The supreme relationship of the human world, marriage, is supplanted with the mystical marriage, a total absorption in God. The devotee then has a love for all humankind engendered by his or her love for God.

In theory that is correct, and perhaps while the world was still in the dark age, a person had to go to that extreme to force freedom upon himself or herself, but did so at a dangerous price. While overcoming their attachment to people and things, it became easy to drop out, to condemn the world of humans and to denigrate the value of their own individual personal selves, or even to kid themselves into thinking they no longer had personal selves.

If the monk or nun succeeded in eliminating all emotion within themselves, they were turning themselves into a kind of separate elemental being, brainwashed automatons. Emotion is the carrier for creativity. No creation is performed without it. It is true that misdirected emotion is a dissipation of the spirit, and one of our most important purposes is to direct our emotional power into creative and healing expressions, but eliminating emotion altogether, even shriveling it out of its relationship to other humans, reduces us to soul shrinkage not soul wholeness. Emotion directed into a fervent love of a true sense of God has to be felt for all people as well, because that is what God is.

In more modern times, fewer persons have physically tried to force themselves into overcoming human emotions, but many have tried to do it mentally. Many students of metaphysical healing religions have so hypnotized themselves into unseeing human conditions that they have lost all compassion. They have tricked themselves into believing they can have the nonattachment of the fourth dimension while they live at the level of their third-dimensional values. Instead of realizing that it is possible to go into meditation and experience the mystical marriage and then come out and respond in one's humanity, they have hidden compassion under a bushel of hypocrisy.

It's easy to see how people were led into this duality. The church in the past put so much emphasis on the human and personal side of Jesus that it often ignored the indwelling Christ in each individual; the metaphysical church came about in order to remind people of their indwelling Godhead. Then, after a while, the pendulum swung too far in the impersonal direction and some metaphysicians threw away the Jesus, the human man, for the Christ.

I personally found this out the hard way. In my panic to storm the gates I forced on myself a kind of monastic life for a number of years. Right in New York City I gave up every emotional and physical attachment of which I could conceive. Though I wasn't off on a mountaintop, the results were much the same. At any rate, I ended up facing the age-old dilemma of loneliness. I didn't realize that I had cut myself off from mankind by my lack of empathy for human problems, and a coldness of soul was brought on by my attempt to rise above emotion.

At the depth of this problem, a spiritually-illumined friend wrote me, "In your aloneness is your allness." If there was anything I did not want to hear, that was it. But I couldn't get it out of my mind until finally I realized what the mystical marriage was. I realized that once I had an absolute experience of the oneness of God I would be whole as never before, and then I would be able to feel for all mankind.

Aloneness is different from loneliness. Aloneness is pure oneness. We experience mystical marriage when our aloneness reaches the point where we stop seeing ourselves as separate beings, cut off from life, and realize our oneness with all.

Each of us, in order to be a whole man and know our man of God, must at some time in our life experience that total absorption in the divine self. We can do it by a mixture of personal discipline, by a retreat where we go off alone for a period, by an experience we have through meditation, by a dark night of the soul, or by none of those ways. Under grace, there is no one way in which the experience of mystical marriage is brought about. There is no law covering it. It will come because we have recognized it; it will come because each of us has dedicated ourself to being a whole man or woman without eliminating any aspect of ourself. The mystical marriage can take place in an instant, a moment no matter how short, of the experience of total absorption in oneness, and each of us is born with the capacity for achieving this mystical marriage.

Perhaps there will be a time when we must deliberately, and even coldly, put the problems of others out of our minds and refuse to acknowledge them for a while. Perhaps we must quote the rather cruel statement Jesus made when he was informed his own mother and brother were outside. He said, somewhat brutally, "Who is my my mother and who is my brother? Those who love the Lord." In other words, "Just because they are my human mother and brother, that doesn't mean a thing. I am not interested in human attachments. My real family are those who have experienced the mystical oneness." As for that, Jesus was often rather cold to human problems, yet on the other hand, he healed and fed the multitudes. He was a whole man.

It is impossible to understand fully a human marriage unless one has caught a glimpse of the mystical marriage—and vice versa.

This mystical marriage has even been explained by science in its own terms. All matter, we learn, is made up of atoms. The only difference between one form and another is the composition or density of the atoms. A rock is a denser composite of atoms than a marshmallow, but basically they are both made up of atoms. We also learn that all atoms are constantly on the move. They go off into the air or turn into other substances. A rock may look the same to the human eye for thousands and thousands of years because each atom is replaced by another atom that looks just the same, but nonetheless, the atoms are constantly coming and going.

Scientists say that there are some 5,000,000,000,-000,000, 000,000,000,000 atoms in one human body, that if these atoms were the size of peas they would form a ten-foot-thick layer around the whole earth and many other planets as well. As these atoms are constantly leaving the body and becoming part of other bodies, in time each one of us has some atoms in our body that were in the bodies of other beings who have long since left the earth.

Each one of us has within us, even humanly, some of the atoms that were in the body of Jesus Christ. By the same token, we have atoms that were in Buddha, Caesar, or even Genghis Khan. Physically, we are married to all other beings. If we open ourselves to that marriage, in time, like yeast that leavens all the dough, that spirit of freedom which was in the Christ or Buddha can leaven us into the purity that was theirs. This material and spiritual union is the true meaning behind the communion service. By communion, we are married to all mankind.

The Marriage Mirror

That's all well and good. Perhaps it helps me to know those absolutes, but far more of my time is spent as my man of earth self. I can experience the God man in a moment, but my days are lived facing problems at the one-to-one level of human relationships. The infinite me may not need anyone or anything, but the infinite me also doesn't think in terms of "me" and "mine"; it doesn't have downs, get lonely, or lose its way.

As a human being at the third-dimensional level, I am not complete and I need other humans to complete me. I need physical contact, mental contact, and spiritual contact with other humans. As a human being, I need the love of at least one other human to form a bridge to infinity. Unless there is another human loving me, I am not linked with mankind and my soul isn't opened to its own creativity at that level.

God is the love I need, but love needs another person to be expressed through at the third-dimensional level. At this level, God cannot be expressed unless love comes through the consciousness of someone in terms of their body, their mind, and their spirit. At this level, there are times when the physical affection of another human is necessary, when the mental guidance of another human is necessary, when the spiritual prayer of another human is necessary.

Though all personal relationships are a kind of partnership, the supreme example and the high point of a personal relationship is marriage. Just as the old morality has broken down in other areas, it has been taking a beating in its application to the institution of marriage as well. If we have a clear, new-day understanding of the purpose or need of marriage, we can set about building a morality of grace for it.

First of all, no human being can be perfectly objective about himself any more than a picture can jump out of its frame and turn around and look at itself. Our human identity is in a constant state of flux, so if we could have a mirror in which to look whenever we need it, we could have some perspective on the state of our humanness. No one needs to tell the actor how he looks in his dressing room, but he needs a director to be his mirror as to how he looks on the stage.

A perfect marriage is one in which two people act as mirrors for each other. Whenever there is doubt, and it can't be cleared up by obtaining release in meditation, another person is needed.

I have known completely dedicated mystics who have found it necessary to leave the silence of their retreats in order to be active in the world. While in the world, each one needed a wife, a husband, or at least a particularly dedicated friend to turn to at times for objectivity about human activities. Perhaps the mystic only lacked help in obtaining objectivity about simple matters, but he needed someone. Often, mysticism made him less objective about material matters than the average person, and he needed a mate who was particularly grounded in an understanding of the level of material manifestation.

Most often, we find that two people end up in a marriage with each supplying what the other lacks, and in this way they are infinite in their togetherness. Each mirrors the other.

Our need for a mirror gives us a clue in choosing a mate. If our mate doesn't have the same potential range in his scale that we do in ours, it is impossible for that person to reflect back an accurate picture of our true being. If the one we couple with is a cracked glass or a clouded mirror, he can do no more than reflect an image of us that is affected by his cracks or cloudiness, and we are not seeing ourselves, our human selves, in a true perspective. Instead he projects his own limitations on to us.

When we have a mate, however, who has the same range of creative, spiritual, or mental interests, one who looks out on life with more or less the same spiritual values that we do, then we can expect that mate to give us back a reliable sense of ourselves. A mate who is riddled by fear, uptight about security, full of judgment, cannot keep from coloring what he or she reflects back.

I am not saying that the person to whom one is drawn is not the right person because, at some particular moment, he or she does not have the qualities necessary to be a mirror. I am only saying that the relationship has not yet reached the marriage stage. In such cases, it might be well for the two people to make conscious efforts to reach a fuller understanding, to give themselves time to grow before getting married. It may only mean that the right time for the marriage just hasn't come yet, but the chances are that two people rushing into a marriage without an awareness of the necessity of their being mirrors for each other might find themselves headed for more down experiences than they wish.

On the other hand, when two people are suited to mirror each other, a wonderful miracle can take place. You know what happens when two mirrors are held up in front of each other. They reflect infinity.

In another way, this capacity to "see" a person is the capacity for love. The quality which marks a relationship as a "love affair" is the ability of the two to view each other with love. Each has the capacity not only to see the true perfect spiritual center of the other person but to judge the human aspect accordingly. Because a person is what the world calls "blindly in love," he or she is not necessarily unaware of the human flaws. It simply means that he or she is aware of the whole person and may be just the right one to enter into a marriage because he or she could reflect back a whole image of the one they love.

A word of warning can go along with the capacity to see wholly or reflect wholly. The more God we see in someone, the more possible it is to find faults because the areas in which one is separated from perfection become more obvious. When we see the potential of another, it is easy to expect too much of that person. That is why, as mirrors, we must take great care not to judge, but only to reflect back the picture.

We all need someone to whom we can turn, someone who will have the strength to show us where we are at the time but who is anchored enough in the spirit not to fall into the old traps of morality, judgment and condemnation. When two people reflect back in the same spirit, they have a spiritual marriage.

The Marriage Responsibility

A successful marriage requires a responsibility, a commitment, that can't be honestly made unless a person loves himself enough not to condemn himself when he is in a down. As long as a person is ashamed to admit being exhausted or out of contact, he can't possibly be honest to the partnership of marriage.

A marriage is a total involvement. Each person brings his whole self into the coupling. Whatever belongs to one belongs to the other. As such, there are not two, only one. Since a marriage under grace is not based on negatives, each partner assumes at all times that his mate is a kind of reserve tank that can be called upon for help whenever one of them feels a shortage of body, mind, or spirit. Humanly speaking, persons alone have to be sure they don't spend too much of their energy or substance because they have no reserve apart from themselves to call upon, but a partnered person can go right out to the limits of his talents and capacities, because he knows his mate will offer sustenance when he is exhausted.

The condition is rather like two astronauts in a capsule searching outer space. When one of the astronauts wants to make a space walk, he leaves the capsule with oxygen in his tank. He knows that he can wander around to the end of his connecting line as long as he leaves himself just enough oxygen to get back to the capsule. There is always a reserve of oxygen left in the capsule waiting for him. Otherwise he could never go to his full limit because he would always have to save some reserve in order to have time to generate some more when he got back.

Well, marriage is like that. As humans, we attain greater capability or capacity by coupling than by being alone, but we also have a responsibility. And that is to keep our companion informed when we ourselves are running out of energy. We go under the assumption that there are reserves ready to recharge us with physical, mental, or spiritual help at all times, so we don't have to remind our partner constantly that we are O.K., any more than we need to remind our loved ones every minute that they are loved. . . they know it. But we do have to let our partner know when we are down or lacking in any area.

We have to let him or her know we are down not only so he or she can offer us help, but also, and most important, so he or she won't spend all of their substance without realizing we have no reserve left, allowing the whole partnership to go dry. That is why the relationship has to be so honest that each partner will tell the other when they are shaky.

Therefore, unless we have seen the necessity of downs, have seen that bad periods have their creative necessity, we cannot take our whole selves into a relationship. Unless we have seen that dark periods are part of the whole and we don't feel guilt in having them, we cannot refrain from trying to hide our downs from others. If we believe downs are bad, we have to admit failure when we have a down, and no one wants to admit failure. It levies too much of a tax on love. As long as we fear that our partner won't love us if we lack in body, mind, or spirit, we are back in old-fashioned darkness. If we don't inform our partner of our shortages, we might betray the partnership. We must remember that our downs allow our partner to give to us, to love us.

A friend of mine, a teacher and lecturer, carried a rather rough schedule of appointments and interviews. He was able to do this because his wife was a good manager, thereby granting him freedom from many business and household matters so that he could channel his energies to the limits of his talent as an author and spiritual guide for others.

One day he had a particularly heavy schedule, with

a public lecture to be given that night as well. So he scheduled time for himself to take a nap and have a meditation before dinner and the lecture. As it turned out, just as he was finishing his list of appointments, appointments requiring him to share of himself in every way, an unannounced visitor arrived who needed his help. He could not refuse. Out went the rest period, and he drew on his own reserves right up until dinner-time.

When he went to the kitchen, there was no dinner on the stove. He found his wife in the bedroom, resting. She informed him that she hadn't felt well all day but she hadn't wanted him to know because she was so angry at herself for having been weak.

Now this is not a dramatic or serious example. My friend had enough inner guidance and reserve to pull himself up, make his own dinner, and unstintingly give of himself to those who came to the lecture. But take a look. His wife certainly never intended to harm him or the partnership, quite the opposite, but her feeling guilty about being tired or sick nevertheless could have made it impossible for her husband to do his best at his lecture. Had he known she was unable to help him, he could have either canceled unnecessary appointments or cut others short. Then he would have had the time for the rest and meditation which he might have needed in order to open himself to be a clear channel for the spirit to work through. As it turned out, this down experience taught them the responsibility to communicate in order to make their marriage an even more total experience of oneness.

In a marriage of grace, there is never John's career or Mary's painting, John's intelligence or Mary's sensitivity. Both partners together make up infinity. They are joined. As all of their body, mind and spirit make up infinity, they work out guidelines with as little "me" or "mine" as possible but with a lot of "our." And when they understand their "our," they form a bridge to all mankind and stretch the family of oneness a bit further.

I can think of no more eloquent or perfect expression of this spirit of total commitment than the one expressed in a hippie wedding ceremony at which I was present. The two who were being joined together were asked to repeat a vow. First the man said, "I promise that, in no matter what temporary condition I find Mary, I will remember she is a sacred and eternal being." After the girl repeated the vow to him he went on to say, "I promise to commit myself with love and candor to the freedom and fulfillment of Mary—body, mind, and soul forever." I can't imagine a more spiritual commitment.

CHAPTER SIX

Contact Morality

"Contact" is one of the most important and exciting words in my vocabulary. I am so aware of the necessity of staying in contact with my own inner source (God), and the necessity of staying in contact with other people, that the first thing I always do when things start going wrong is to check to see where and how I may have broken contact. It's an exciting word because now that I know I am connected in one way or another with every person in the world, I find it "groovy" to understand the contact I have with others and to find my responsibility to that contact. Because I have a responsibility (remember, response-ability) to every person in the human family, I must find out how to respond to each one. Some of my contacts are more personal and involved than others; so there are different things I must do in order to keep from breaking contact.

To understand contact I need a morality of grace; I have to understand what maintaining contact means. First of all, contact has to do with what is in my consciousness rather than something physical.

To explain what keeping in contact means, let us return to our analogy of the vine for a minute. A leaf, like an individual, is connected to a stem. Perhaps, as in a marriage, two leaves grow on a single stem, and the stem is in turn attached to a twig where there are several marriages forming a kind of family. Then the twig is attached to a branch making up a whole city of families. The branch is connected to a limb of the vine. This branch with all its cities and all their families forms a kind of nation, and the limb along with other limbs ties into the trunk of the tree, joining the whole of humankind. As individuals, we are like leaves joined to the vine of all humanity.

Whatever affects the vine affects each individual leaf, and to some extent whatever affects each leaf affects the vine. When a leaf gets disconnected from the vine, it naturally withers and dies. When a leaf get dis-eased, it could spread its dis-ease through the whole vine, so it most likely is rejected by the vine before much damage is done to the whole.

The most fragile connection point is that point where the individual is joined to the vine. That's why the number one responsibility for each individual is to maintain his own health and keep his own contact. After that, there is a whole chain of responsibilities necessary to maintain contact with our mate, then our children, our family, our city, our nation, and finally the whole of mankind.

It is easy to find out what maintaining contact in a relationship means. All we have to do is ask ourselves what we want from the particular relationship. In order to keep the connection alive, we have to give to a relationship what we want from it.

Say, for instance, that you have a "once-a-month friendship" with someone. You want that person to cross your path at least once every month or so, catch up with mutual interests, and maybe offer you a laugh or two, then go his or her own way. If you don't check in with that friend yourself every month, if you are not interested in his or her doings, and if you don't remember an amusing experience to pass on to him or her, you are not doing your part and are breaking contact.

The key lies in the word "contact." Our integrity of human relationships depends on our ability to keep from being tricked into disconnecting our consciousness from those to whom we want to be connected. Of course, some relationships imply a much deeper contact level than others, but there is a guideline we can use when we are contemplating an action and want to see what that action entails. We ask, "can I commit myself to this activity and stay healthy, spiritually and physically? Will the commitment cause me to break contact with someone to whom I want to stay connected?" If the answer is yes, then we ask, "can I do this without breaking contact with my marriage?" Once more, if the answer is yes, we ask the same question on down the line about family, business, partnership, society, the whole of mankind. If some action we are planning might possibly put a strain on any commitment down the line, we can ask ourselves if the value of the action is worth it. If we don't think the plan is worth disconnecting, we can drop it.

In our morality of grace, there are some suggestions we can follow to help us stay in contact. We should never go into any relationship without realizing to what degree we are being hooked up with others. We can ask to what degree we want our consciousness tied up with theirs. Naturally, the supreme involvement is the total relationship of marriage. Such absolute commitment requires that contact be kept intact at all times. It's not a matter of clock time, because two people who are super-sensitive to each other can develop an inner ear or spirit link with their mate so that they know if they are in contact even though they might not see each other for days.

Another commitment which many enter without enough serious consideration is the relationship of a business partnership. Though a business associate in not a part of one's immediate family, he or she directly affects the well-being of the whole family. *Whenever your good is dependent on another person, place, or thing you are psychically hooked up with them.* Through a business, a man expects to feed himself and his family, if he has one. The physical, mental, and spiritual conditions of the partnership will doubtless affect the outcome. Once a commitment is made to a partnership, both partners are humanly and psychically hooked up. They take on each other's vibrations and carry a mutual load.

Before entering a partnership, we can ask ourselves: Am I and my future partner ready and able to commit ourselves in the same manner and to the same degree? Does my partner have the capacity to operate with the kind of spirit which I must operate to be healthy? Does my partner understand his responsibility to this commitment as I do? Is he taking his whole self into it as I am intending to do? And most of all, am I ready to commit my own health and that of my family to this partner? If the answers lack a rather strong degree of affirmation, it would be wise to look further before hooking up with him.

Any business we connect up with, whether it is a partnership or a corporation, affects our contact with life in all kinds of ways. Involvement in a business with a product which is designed for destroying human life, poisoning the atmosphere, or for messing up people's head with drugs, affects our own head. If we become involved with mentally or physically poisonous products, we haven't realized what that contact will do to us. The outside and the inside are one. A person is one with the thing he produces.

Though family and business commitments are the most serious ones we enter, every relationship right on down the line to the most casual implies a degree of hook-up. Some hook-ups affect our security to a large degree, others to a small degree. If we want a lot out of a relationship we have to be prepared to give a lot to it. We must always enter a hook-up with the same degree of importance that we place on what we want from the relationship. When we want little from a contact, we are not committed to stay in close contact, but if we want much from a relationship, we must be prepared to do our part to keep the contact strong.

If another person wants to enter a degree of contact with us, or if we see them unconsciously assuming a commitment which we are not able to enter or do not want to be involved with, it is up to us to level with them and to let them know we are not going to become involved with any commitment we are not prepared to fulfill.

Threats to Contact

We can sit down right now and go over our commitments to see if unintentional disconnects or wrongly understood contacts have put a strain on our present relationships. After we have asked ourselves what we expect from a friendship or relationship, we can see how we may have betrayed that relationship by breaking contact.

In friendship, simple friendship from which we want no more than mutual appreciation, we betray the friendship when we remove ourselves by judging the other person. We break contact when we try to maneuver the other person as though he is separate from our own selves; we disconnect when we try to use the friend for our personal advantage or to fulfill our own personal desire without thinking of his or her needs and likes.

A university student I know had built up a really beautiful relationship with his grandmother. There was an amazing lack of generation gap. Each respected the other, and each was wide open to face life without judging in terms of the old morality, but something happened that gave the relationship a temporary setback.

One day the student called his grandmother, who lived a few miles from the university, and asked if he could come to dinner. The grandmother responded honestly and said she was a little low that evening and thought it probably wasn't the best time, but the grandson reminded her it was her birthday. She acquiesced and agreed to cook dinner for him and a couple of his friends.

Now, from the conversation, the rules of the game were established. He knew that his grandmother needed support that night, and he had implied his trip was for the purpose of sharing the personal celebration of her birthday. As it turned out, he and his friends got to the house and went straight to the game room. One of them had brought along some marijuana that had been given to him. With curiosity, the three students, who were certainly not old hands at smoking pot, tried it out and succeeded in getting stoned.

In the meantime, grandmother was in the kitchen spending her energy cooking for three hungry men. When dinnertime arrived, they came in giggling under the influence of the marijuana and, instead of communicating with the grandmother or even acknowledging her presence, they gobbled at the food. The grandmother was sensitive enough to realize that something unusual was taking place. She was honest enough to show her annoyance.

Since the boy's relationship with his grandmother had

always been an honest one, and he had confidence that though she might not agree with all the things he did, she would not judge him but would offer him her advice and understanding, he explained what he and his friends had done.

Grandmother blew up. You might think that she blew up because her grandson was using a drug, or because he had dared to use it in her home, but that wasn't the case. She sensed that they had broken contact, so she demanded that the boys leave the house. In fact, she put on quite a scene herself.

The grandson returned to his school, knowing that something serious had taken place in his relationship with someone who was very important to him, not because of a family relationship but because of the love and understanding he needed. Since he was one of those young people who are looking for a new kind of guideline based on a new morality, he spent days struggling with the answer to his disastrous evening.

Finally, he came up with the truth. He had broken contact with grandmother because he had used her, used her to cook dinner for him, without giving her something in return. And he had also disconnected himself by smoking marijuana while she was not on the same trip, thus making contact impossible. He realized that her actions were not just an old-fashioned fear of drugs but were honest reactions to the betrayal of his deliberate disconnect.

The story has a happy ending. The realization of what he had done made him visit his grandmother again, at which time he vowed never to use her without giving in return, never to visit unless he expected to communicate. He also saw how drugs had tricked him into a violation of love, into breaking contact.

I guess we have all experienced the annoyance of being in the presence of a friend who is drinking when we are not. The alcohol affects his vibration or psyche, and he starts communicating at a level where we are not. He breaks contact with us. Our annoyance isn't a judgment of the drinking, or shouldn't be; it is over the recognition that he has disconnected from the commitment of friendship for that moment.

In the parent-child relationship, there are many ways we break contact without realizing it. They are not just those of a child's acceptance of security from the parents without the child's fulfilling his side of the bargain. Often parents disconnect from their child by betraying the growth of the child without realizing what they are doing. Children need a chance to grow by stretching. The young come to a time when they need to rebel in order to grow strong, need to test themselves against tough goals. If the parents always agree, always make it easy, always let their children do anything they want, they don't make it necessary for the young to dig deep within themselves and learn. Instead of keeping contact, the parents disconnect from their part of the relationship by not helping the child stretch.

Perhaps old-fashioned fathers were too tough on their sons, but this often made their sons strong. They had to become strong enough to stand on their own two feet. When parents make it too easy for their children, it is because they fear and are insecure themselves. This lack of self-love is an actual break of contact with their children. A common mistake is the belief that the young want it *easy*. They don't. They want it *honest*.

There can be a disconnect in the relationship with a teacher or religious instructor. We break contact when we don't level with him or her, when we withhold our true feelings or thoughts. We disconnect from a teacher when we give him or her lip service but don't try to practice their teaching. We disconnect from the relationship when we take without giving.

We connect in a relationship when we use our strengths and energies with consideration of others and their needs. We connect when we fulfill our commitments. We connect when we are sensitive enough to keep in touch with others, when we remember small pleasures that delight them, when we answer our mail. In short, we connect in a relationship when we communicate or when we create a situation which makes communication possible. Anything that assures a connect is an *up*.

Candoring

When we feel that we are about to break contact with someone and want to avoid it, we can do several things —things which involve our whole selves.

First, we can use our minds for better understanding; we can be candid. As Websters dictionary says, to be candid is to be "frank, outspoken, open, sincere, without reservation, disguise or subterfuge, straightforward, honest and impartial." That's quite a bill. We cannot even begin to approach real candor without applying our whole selves.

However, while our man of God self is trying to make its inner contact for guidance, our man of earth self can sit down with our friend, member of our family, or associate with whom we are in danger of losing contact, in an effort to level with that person and be as candid as possible. If he can do the same, perhaps an unintentional disconnect can be avoided.

That act of attempting total communication with another person is rather like an act of mutual grokking. It means a lot more than just reasoning; it means more than analyzing facts. Mutual grokking requires an honesty about oneself and a willingness to offer oneself with faith. When everything is out in the open and ignorance leaves, love is reestablished.

When we arrive at the realization that it is vitally necessary for us to be candid in our relationships with others and for our friends to be candid with us, we keep in contact. So let's take the work "candor," a noun, and turn it into an active verb. Let's call the act of being candid "candoring."

Whenever a shadow comes over any of our relationships, say, "Let's candor each other," meaning: Let's groove on each other, let's open our hearts with love, let's see that any lack of communication is not due to lack of love but because some ignorance is trying to insinuate itself on our friendship.

There is one catch to candoring. Like grokking, it can't be performed by people who are still living under the law of judgment. Candoring is purely a part of the life of a revolutionary. Anyone who still has to judge in terms of bad and good, in terms of separateness, can't candor. You see, we do indeed use the mind as part of candoring, so if the mind is still trying to be the whole show, if the mind is full of judgment, it can't candor. By the same token, while we are using the mind for candoring, we are candoring with our spirits, and we are offering our bodies to the act.

The spirit of candoring is a positive one or it isn't candoring. We candor not to prove a point, not to get our way, not to resist an evil, but to keep truth present so love can flow freely. Candoring is the act of deliberately meeting in person with someone for the realization of oneness by communicating.

The responsibility for candoring is two-sided. Older people, in candoring with the young, need to let go of their positions of authority and see themselves free of age, as ageless as the one they are trying to candor with. They must keep an inner ear constantly tuned to the spirit of the meeting and the vibration or feeling of it. They must make every attempt to leave yesterday out, as well as their concepts of bad and good.

The young have to try to candor with the old. All too often they have been slapped down by the old, so they have stopped trying to candor. They have to realize that it is often harder, not easier, for the old to candor.

The old have more to lose. They are carrying more mental baggage and have more theories to defend. So the young have to keep trying, have to educate their parents to what candoring means, since candoring or grokking is new to this generation.

We have to realize that in being candored, we are apt to hear some things that make us uncomfortable, and that we must bear the discomfort, writing it off as one of the costs of a real and vital relationship.

When the young just shake their heads and refuse to speak, when they feel unable to candor because they don't have enough words to use or they feel tongue-tied, they are not doing their part as revolutionaries. They must deliberately ask for candoring with their friends and parents and make every effort to offer their whole selves. They must connect.

It seems incredible that we have to be reminded that we need to communicate and keep in contact with each other, but we do, and now that we understand what it means to be whole, we have to remember that communication has many sides. When communication or contact breaks down, it is like a red light signaling us where to put our constructive energies. After all, sometimes even disconnects are necessary for health. You prune a tree at times in order to make it healthier. Don't forget, right now we are in a transitional period. We break contact in many ways that we haven't recognized in the past. Each time we bump into a disconnect, we can grok it; then if it involves other people, we can candor with them and reinforce the connection. Eventually the light will shine strong and solid and we will stay in contact.

The Energy of Love

In order to understand disconnects in an absolute sense, we have to understand energy in an absolute way. In the last chapter, I said that in absolute terms no one ever sees you or me. We are that which is happening through the body. We are the flow of energy. Every moment, energy is flowing. In order to know us, someone has to see us as energy rather than as body.

Modern physicists have done a remarkable job of scientifically proving that man isn't body, that we are more accurate when we don't see people in physical terms. Until now physics was constructed on the belief that matter existed, but most advanced modern physicists have discarded the old theories based on matter and have supplanted them with theories based on the knowledge that everything is energy. Their advanced theorems are based on the fact that regardless of what the misguided visual sense beholds, we are only seeing energy formed. No bodies, no things, all energy.

Actually, the mystics have said the same thing for thousands of years. Even now Christian Science and other metaphysical teachings are predicated on the idea that everything is spirit—or energy formed. When spiritual contact is broken, its appearance as a body gets sick. When the flow of energy is short-circuited, we become disconnected from the true self.

Another way of explaining energy is to equate everything in terms of vibration. Vibration is only the movement of energy. Many young, in a kind of subconscious realization that everything is vibration, often talk about places and people in terms of vibration. They say, "The vibration of that place was down," or, "He sends out bad vibes." In comprehending life as vibration or energy, the young are showing their capacity to relate to the world in terms of its unity and wholeness. "Vibration" is not just a slang term for expressing old-fashioned judgments. It can be used to point out that contact is intact or has been broken, that someone is experiencing an up or a down.

In the past, we often sensed things by vibration but didn't consciously recognize we were doing it. We said, "My first impressions are always right," or, "I should have followed my first impression." At first, we sensed the vibration of a person or situation. But often we let our minds think us out of following our feelings. Our minds clouded the truth with their judgments.

Contact morality depends a great deal on our capacity to see ourselves in terms of energy or vibration. If we do, we can find how we have unintentionally misdirected our energies.

Since man is body, mind, and spirit, he has three kinds of energy. There is the plain physical energy of the body, the energy he needs to make his body perform. There is mental energy; the act of thinking uses mental energy. And there is psychic or spiritual energy, needed to keep man in contact with his source of being. A disruption of any of these energies causes us to lose contact.

Most people are very aware of their physical and mental energies. They take great pains to keep from wearing themselves out physically so they won't feel miserable and become overexhausted. They know better than to work for too long a time without resting or to spend too much time with people who physically exhaust them. Most people realize they have only a certain amount of mental energy. They are aware that a few hours of hard mental work can be more exhausting than many hours of physical labor. They avoid being around people whose minds are uncomfortably overactive. Many businessmen realize they have to give their mind a rest, so they take time off to play golf. Their golf is a necessity for wholeness.

Until now, however, we have not generally understood or recognized our psychic or spiritual energy, so we haven't realized the importance of protecting it. We have let people psychically drain us and we have let ourselves spend too much time in places with a spiritually down vibration, not realizing that we were being used up spiritually. Just because places and people didn't hurt us mentally or physically we thought we were safe, but actually our spirits were being affected. Of course, if we are strong enough, we can go anywhere without danger because when we feel ourselves getting brought down we can recognize it and leave. At times we might be so full of spiritual energy that we can lift a down person or place into our high vibration.

Meditation, which we discuss later, is the main way

to build up spiritual energy. Jesus showed us this by his own example. When he found himself spiritually drained, he knew he could no longer help those who needed his strength, so he went off to the mountaintop to be recharged. Buddha also taught that meditation was the way to recharge.

I could have said that Jesus and Buddha meditated to get recharged with love. Spiritual energy and love are the same thing. Of all the energies in the world, love is by far the most powerful. A loss of love can cause the greatest disconnect, but its presence has the capacity to harmonize, to build, to create, and to connect like no other energy. In fact, love is the energy which will one day save the world.

Man has never been able to understand love because he has seen it as an emotion or a thing, and it isn't. *Love is an energy*, an invisible energy. It is the very essence of energy; it is cosmic or spiritual energy expressed visibly. Love is the only energy capable of harmonizing or connecting all of mankind into oneness.

Look at common ordinary friendship, for instance. Friendship unites people. Through friendship, the energy of love is used to bind people together. Through a sense of love energy, man stops being alone and self-centered. He finds himself joined to others and to the family of mankind—purely through the magnetic force of the energy of love.

Because love is the most powerful and valuable energy, the only one which can save us and therefore the whole world, we must take every precaution not to do anything to jeopardize our ability to love. By that I mean if we dissipate our spirit by pointlessly drifting into down associations which cause us to squander our capacity to love, we are not directing love for the purpose of union with others.

In an absolute sense, God is love. In a personal sense, love is the energy of God when it is seen in personal terms. They are the same; one is unknowable because it is infinite, and the other is recognizable because it is expressed in a finite way. We experience God when we experience formless love, but at the third-dimensional level, we can only love God when we love our neighbor. To waste our energy of love by misdirecting it is to waste our contact with God, the ultimate disconnect.

Under law, as Paul says, "wickedness in high places" has to do with the mind and its control over a person. Under grace, "wickedness in high places" has to do with the dissipation of the energy of love. When we place ourselves in a position where we dissipate our psychic energy in such a way that it brings on a disconnect from our responsibilities to ourselves, our families and mankind, we are in the worst of downs.

It takes great energy to candor, including the energy of love, so we must constantly stand watch on our energies. Without falling under the old morality, we can at any time check in with our whole selves to see if we are letting any of the three aspects of our personal energy run low. If so, something is out of balance, and we can feel or listen for ways to repair it. We can consciously do this—in fact, we *must* consciously do it—if we wish to stay in contact with wholeness.

We can consciously look at every person, place, thing, or happening and see it in terms of energy, of the three energies. The list is infinite, and we may take many years defining the new world in terms of energy, in freeing the world from a material concept of life.

CHAPTER SEVEN

The Puzzle of Sex and Drugs

Ever since man started trying to put together the jigsaw puzzle of his human existence, sex has been the most confusing piece of the puzzle. He couldn't ignore sex, but he couldn't make it fit into the puzzle without forcing it into place by rigid laws. He knew that sex had him trapped, but he didn't realize that if he saw the true meaning and purpose of sex it would slip naturally into place. Instead of sex being his problem, it would help him finish the whole puzzle—whatever can bind a person can also free him.

Sex has been man's most powerful problem because it deals with man's most powerful energy—love. The energy of love expressed in physical terms is the energy of sex. As I said earlier, love is the energy which will eventually unite the whole world, just as in personal terms it expresses itself in the uniting of two people into oneness.

Love is a miracle. It's *the* miracle. Whatever bridges between the invisible spirit and the material form is the miracle, and that miracle takes place every time the sex act is performed with spiritual union, love, and commitment. Through the sex act, the fourth dimension can be brought into the third dimension. When the sex act is no more than a physical phenomenon alone, the miracle does not happen.

The sex act performed by our parents didn't give us visible form by itself. It took a spark. Something had to light the third-dimensional fire. Through sex that fourth-dimensional spark comes to the surface and the word is made flesh. The rest of the time it stays hidden in the invisible. That's the miracle of life.

The spark, the miracle, is given to us not only for procreation but also for *re*-creation or regeneration. Our creative drive can be used to generate more being—a baby, a work of art, something that will make the world free—or to regenerate those who are already here, to fill them with life and vitality. Generation and regeneration are two blossoms on the same bush. Both charge people with new life.

The energy of life expressed through sexual love can be directed toward making the world more sensitive to beauty, to joy, and ultimately to the procreation of the spiritual instinct in people. Through the energy of love expressed sexually, men and women can draw others into a more living sense of the spiritual capacities of their natures. In fact, when sex comes from love, it can open up a person to his or her spiritual capacities. Sex can be a valuable part of fulfilling the person spiritually.

Be fearing sex, by condemning sex, and by not realizing how spiritually important it is to people, many have been deprived of the generative and regenerative values as well as the spiritual link involved in the physical expression of the energy of love. If humankind is to be whole, we must spiritualize sex. We must eliminate the duality of separating sex from the miracle of life. We must understand sex and not be confused by it.

It isn't altogether our fault that we have been confused about sex in the past. Because we lived by law, we couldn't see that what was adding to wholeness one minute might be a disconnect the next. Marriage had a different sexual purpose in the past. Now the main purpose of marriage has changed. In the past, we were a people-needing world; we needed to populate the world, so the prime purpose of sexual relations in the past was for reproduction inorder to populate the world.

That isn't so any longer. We do not need greater populations. The need now is for the energy of sexual love to be used for making the world more sensitive to beauty, to joy, to the fulfilling and regeneration of our loved ones. As I said, sex can draw two people into a more living sense of the spiritual capacities of their natures. When love is present, sex can be a way of lifting and healing.

Today we are ready to communicate at deeper levels of our being than ever before, so sex can be a supreme expression of soul communication. When two people bring their whole selves into sex, a circle is completed and the same miracle which brought them into the world as babies can lift them into spiritual freedom.

That is what sex can do when it is in its right place,

doing what it is "for". But if the circle isn't complete, if there isn't wholeness, sex can cause a disconnect. We can't just rush out and bring all the fulfillment of which love sexually expressed is capable to the world. Unless the inherent miracle is vastly respected and nourished, it can instead seem to separate a person from his or her source of life, can anchor him or her more to the third dimension and the material level.

We are not bodies. We are consciousness with bodies. More than any other experience in life, sex can either free us from body sense or it can make us feel we are bodies rather than the spirit in or as the body.

Most of us are familiar with the ways our thoughts and feelings on sex can bring us down to a material sense of life. For instance, if people are sexually frustrated, if their minds have tricked them into thinking they are not complete without having some sexual contact with a particular person, at a particular time, place, or frequency, if they desire a relationship with someone who lacks love for them, they become terribly aware of their own bodies. Their bodies become prisons, torturing them; they feel cut off from life. When a sexually frustrated person becomes extremely body-conscious, he certainly can't get free enough from his body awareness to meditate and achieve a fourth-dimensional experience of pure bodiless spirit.

But unless we want to revert to the old duality of law, we must realize that at times even sexual frustration has its purpose. Unless we have fully arrived at a realization of our wholeness, we may become mired down in stagnation without sexual frustration pushing us into getting involved, pushing us into the necessity of finding the truth.

Remember, we are talking about the third dimension now. At the fourth dimension there is only Oneness, and at that level there are no problems. What we need is a morality of grace applying to sex which can instruct us in the basic principles for sexual involvement at the human level. Then we can know when sex is fulfilling itself as a means of uniting us with wholeness or when it leads us to breaking contact with ourselves and others.

The key to a morality of sex is the remembrance that sex is basically the energy of love. We have a lot more of this energy of life than we may imagine; we often spend or waste it without realizing we are doing so. When sex is fulfilled with love, there is no strain put on our contact—exactly the opposite, our contact is strengthened—but sex without love can be a spending of the energy of life without receiving in return.

We haven't yet grown to the point where we consciously understand this life energy; often we are not consciously aware when we have used too much of ourselves. One of the ways we know if we have depleted ourself is if our sense of joy is down, if our creativity is dulled, if we feel tempted to fight the world, if our appetite for the spirit is low. When that is the case, the continuance of short-circuited sex can just take us further down, but by the same token, real love can restore us. It's not a matter of good and bad; it's a matter of knowing ourselves and the part love plays in our life.

Most often when we think we want sex, we really want love. When we are attracted to someone physically we think we are turned on sexually, but what we are really starved for is love, the energy of love. Even if we were to have a physical relationship with the person we desire, we would still feel frustrated and unfulfilled unless the circle of love was complete.

When two people who no longer love each other are forced into the same marriage bed by the old morality of the marriage license, the two are spending themselves without receiving the regenerative good that their contact would have for them if love were present. On the other hand, when two people see the God within each other, recognize love in each other, are committed to the wholeness of each other and express the energy of love in a mutual relationship, they are truly married, license or not.

Love is not a matter of time. It doesn't have to take a year or a month or any set length of time in order to feel and recognize mutual love, but it is a very tricky matter. We all too often get desire mixed up with love, and we can jump into a down sexual experience mistakenly thinking we have qualified, that we love.

So what guidelines can we use as man of earth? To begin with, we can make two tests. First, in pursuing the steps which may lead up to a close and rewarding union with another person, we can ask ourselves if we and they are able to take our whole selves into the relationship. We are body, mind, and spirit. We know we can take our body into a relationship because we feel attracted to the other person. We know we can take our mind into it if the other person is someone with whom we can share thoughts and interests, even spiritually-minded thoughts. We know if the vibration or spirit of that person is the kind of spirit we want to have union with, if his or her spirit is loving and capable of taking flight.

The second necessity is the most important one. For sex to be in the right spirit, there must be *commitment*. Sexual relations without commitment, without the commitment to give, unite, or make whole, become a separating rather than uniting experience. Commitment has to do with the *self* of the other person. Commitment is made to the oneness of self—not inferior or superior, but one. Finally, commitment has to do with the miracle that is contained in a relationship.

One doesn't have to be committed in order to derive pleasure from sex, but commitment is necessary if growth is to occur and if true joy is to be experienced.

Understanding Our Sex Selves

In committing ourselves to the fulfillment of another person, we can start by realizing that we are potentially one with infinity. Each of us has a degree of both male and female qualities within us. When we reach infinity there won't be any degrees, we will be all, but on the way we have more of one quality and less of the other. A man usually has many more male tendencies in him than female, and a woman has more female than male.

In the regular course of things, a person is attracted to another person whom they feel is strong in the areas in which he or she is weak, and vice versa. Each person is reaching out to wholeness and is drawn to another person whose qualities will balance theirs. Extremes attract extremes, and as balance is reached, a balanced person is attracted to another balanced person.

That sounds awfully clinical, but we can actually see an example of it in the changes that have taken place in our society. Today many of the young, who are realizing a greater degree of the infinity or androgeny of their being than their predecessors, look alike, act alike, and even dress alike. Many of the stores where the young purchase their clothing are unisex stores, offering clothing for sale which can be worn by either men or women. In every way the young today accept a high sense of equality.

On the other hand, in the guise of equality, a number of people have confused equality with sameness. This confusion has led to much frustration. More simply, when we do not know ourselves fully, we often feel a confusion of roles. Man often doesn't know what it means to be man, and woman doesn't always know what it means to be woman. When man understands which of his actions are predicated on his male instincts and which are predicated on his female ones, he can be clear about his responsibilities and how to fulfill them. When he is called on to express his male qualities, he can do so without confusing the roles. The same is true for women.

The confusion of roles has mainly to do with a confusion of strengths and abilities, but it also manifests itself sexually and causes problems in marital relations, because in accepting the belief that we should be all one way or all the other, we leave no room for the roles to change from time to time in a natural fashion.

We must be aware of what the male and female qualities represent in order to know how to fully be ourselves. Traditionally, the male in a person represents the creative spirit, the invisible source which creates out of the imagination rather than from the visible body. The female side is that which represents the word made flesh, the material or visible which is seen in ways you can see and touch. These two qualities are reaching out toward each other, trying to join, like two pieces of metal being magnetically attracted. They are not duality. They are polarity—two aspects of the same.

If the male side of us doesn't recognize that the female side is the symbol of the earth, the love of the visible world with all its shortcomings and problems, we don't comprehend our true love. We spend ourselves wastefully without making the world a better place in which to live. That is why the male in us has to find out all of the secrets of science and the universe. We must love the world, the female.

If the female side in each of us doesn't let go of its worship of material substance and wholly give itself by recognizing the God within, the creative spark, the male consciousness, we spend our energies by placing a false value on material security and don't love the male.

Because society didn't love itself in terms of wholeness, the confusion about homosexuality grew. As we all have a degree of both the male and the female within the infinity of our being we all feel a degree of affection or attraction to members of our own sex. This attraction is most often no more physical than a warm handshake or a loving pat on the cheek, and not something we recognize as being sexual, but it is a form of physical attraction. When women admire each other's figures or men horse around enjoying physical contact in some form of athletic competition, they are expressing this attraction.

In the past, if a man felt consciously attracted to his fellow man, or wanted to openly show affection, he was forced into dishonesty. He either had to refuse to admit to himself that he had any affection or attraction, or if he admitted it to himself, he had to think he was homosexual. Since our society condemned homosexuality as being "queer" or "perverted," he was tempted to think of himself as sick, as a sick homosexual, cut off from society. By believing he was sick, he broke his contact with wholeness and was sick.

When a man is unable to have a lasting relationship with a woman, or when he lets sexual frustration keep him from becoming attached, his alienation may stem from the same cause which has kept a number of people from making a commitment. In an obviously materially changing time, there is a fear of material responsibility, fear of being swamped by material needs. Since having a family represents material involvement, a man may turn away from contact with women or from being attached because he doubts his ability to take on more responsibility. If so, he turns to promiscuity or to other men for sex because he feels that this way he isn't threatened.

Because man, in the male sense, dominates materiality, some women become frigid or turn to lesbianism out of fear. They fear being materially destroyed by man in a world in which men are unleashing such powers of destruction. Because of a lack of belief in herself, a woman may be afraid of sexual relations with a man through which she might be called on to give birth to wholeness.

What I am talking about has nothing to do with gender. Each of us have both male and female qualities or energies. The important thing is that two people offer each other wholeness and commitment.

Never forget, everything that appears at the third-dimensional level is an effect. Even the sex act is an effect; sex itself is an effect. When we believe that an effect has power, when we give it power, we are not free. I guess if there is anything "bad" about sex, it is that it has the power to trick us into believing there is a cause other than our spirit of love.

When we act out of desire which isn't predicated on love, we are grabbing at the fruit of life. We may even be cutting down the tree to get at the fruit. Sex is the fruit of love. It's the reward for having the capacity to love.

Doing a Natural

Ever since man discovered his body, he has been confused about sex. Now that man is discovering his soul, a new confusion has risen, confusion about drugs. Drugs have been around for a long time without any massive concern on the part of the public, but drugs, all the way from aspirin to crack, are woven into our way of life, and mankind is having growing pains finding out what drugs are all about.

Nothing takes place by accident. If drugs have taken on importance, it is because they represent something significant that is taking place in the inner consciousness of mankind. After all, drugs themselves are effects. They are the result of a need man had within or he wouldn't have manufactured them. Like anything man can identify at the level of phenomena, drugs are a part of the third dimension. We could wear out typewriters compiling lists of bads and goods, of laws to regulate, of theories and opinions about drugs, but that wouldn't help us form a morality of grace pertaining to them. We must not sit in judgment, but rather try to understand them.

Though psychedelic drugs have been used for centuries by some American Indians and different cultures all over the world, they are a relatively new phenomenon for society in general because now is the first time that our society has awakened to the fact that we are not necessarily prisoners of our bodies and minds, that we have a soul which is demanding the light.

Mankind, and particularly youth, is not going to sit back and wait for freedom. Unless the youth are presented with a better way of breaking the mind's hold on them, unless they are convinced that there is another way of self-expansion which won't just bind them back into patterns of judgment and self-denial, they will explore what drugs can do, because obviously drugs can drastically liberate one's head from the brainwashing it has been conditioned by—fortunately or unfortunately, both the good and the bad brainwashing.

Remember the old vaudeville song, "How are you going to keep 'em down on the farm after they've seen Paree?" Well, it is rather like that. Many today have caught a glimpse of the spirit, a glimpse of the high at which humans will one day live. How can anyone expect them to now sit still and be satisfied with a structure of society which asks—no, demands—that they live in a low simply because society doesn't know what freedom and highs are?

Whereas Daddy and Mommy drink whiskey to give them the courage to compete, to go on the make, to cope with the values of a competitive society, Junior takes drugs which give him the courage and way to resist the machine and not have to compete, not have to conform to the hypocrisies of that society.

If Daddy and Mommy want Junior to stop being involved in drugs, they had better realize what their side of the bargain is. Not only do Daddy and Mommy have to stop leaning on their own pep pills, tranquilizers, sleeping pills, and martinis, but they have to restructure their whole society and eliminate all the false values they want Junior to swallow—along with the pills. Then, to top that off, Daddy and Mommy had better come across with a true awareness of God. They had better not only offer Junior a religion which can show him a natural way to live in the height of spirit but also show Junior that Junior too can attain it. A big order. A staggering order. But I have a suspicion that Junior would gladly jump in and help, give up drugs or anything else, if he had even a hint that Dad and Mom were starting to build such a life and religion.

Anyone who thinks that the young have turned to drugs out of some kind of perversity, or out of the pure and simple physical desire relevant to drink and other material indulgences of the past, is wrong. Both consciously and subconsciously, the young realize that their true life is not bound up in body and mind alone, that they live wherever their consciousness reaches and they are on a trip to find themselves in the most far-out distances of their awareness potential. When they are shown ways to explore themselves without drugs they are all too delighted to give them up, but not until.

Ways are coming in the Now Age. That's part of the ultimate revolution. And with these ways, a new expression is added to the "head" language of the past. Experiencing a high without drugs was called doing a "natural."

Many years ago, I was present at a group when a girl came into the room with a big smile on her face, her head obviously in heaven. Someone commented, "What's she on?" and the answer came, "Nothing. She's doing a natural."

Almost everyone I know wants ultimately to do it natural. That's our birthright. We have within us, within our own soul and capacities, the spiritual muscles for having a natural high.

None of us should ever want to stay on an absolute

continuous high. While we are still on the earth we need some lows to groove on in order to fuel the highs, but we will learn more and more how to arrive at a natural high and how to keep our heads there.

The Energy of Drugs

Any morality of grace for the new day is involved with maintaining contact rather than judging; in order to understand how we lose contact, we have to understand the energy of drugs.

As we know, every effect represents some kind of energy which in one way or the other keeps us in contact with ourselves and others. We know that alcohol and food primarily affect our mental and physical energies. After a night of heavy drinking or after overindulging in rich foods, we are down and heavy in body and mind. Our overindulgence has drawn too heavily on our mental and physical energies.

Well, drugs basically work on a different energy. That's both their appeal and their stumbling block. Drugs directly affect our spiritual or psychic energies. They appeal because they stimulate our spiritual forces. They make us aware of our spiritual potential and the highs of which man is capable. But they can also drain those energies.

Sex and drugs have been the two things most feared by mankind because they involve man's two most vital energies. Sex involves the energies of life, representing creativity, material contact, and human love; drugs affect the energies involved in spirituality and God contact, or the love of God.

An abundance and flow of the vital energies can lift

us from material and mental bondage into the freedom of spirit; a lack or shortage of these energies leaves us earthbound and heavy.

Mystics have told us for centuries that there are certain key centers in the body, the shakras, representing all levels of being from the most animal and primary to the ultimate and spiritual. They say that those who achieve contact in meditation touch all of those centers at various stages of their meditation. Now medical science, as well as Edgar Cayce, has revealed that each of these centers corresponds to our various nerve centers and glands in the body.

The spiritual center, the mystics have always said, is between our eyes (the third eye). The Brahman, or spiritual caste, salutes this center by wearing a red dot on the forehead between the eyes.

This center corresponds to vital glands in our head which regulate our whole body and spirit. Drugs directly affect this center.

Drugs affect the glands which regulate our flow of adrenaline and the secretions of similar glands such as the pineal and pituitary. They do it in various ways. For instance, marijuana stimulates the flow of adrenaline. LSD is a kind of imitation adrenaline which the regulatory forces in our body attack, trying to keep our adrenaline in check while our own adrenaline stimulates us into an unnaturally high state.

No matter how we are affected by drugs, it is actually our own adrenaline which turns us on. The kind of intoxication we feel when we experience joy, when we are stimulated by great art or spiritual exaltation, comes because for some reason those experiences have caused our glands to naturally produce something like a drug. For some reason, meditation results in a flow of adrenaline. In his book, *The Varieties of Religious Experience*, William James wrote that all great saints or religious leaders had one thing in common—they were all highly adrenal people. In other words, they were turned on. They were high on the "natch," by turning on naturally.

At any rate, there seems to be some physical relation, some bridge, between the source of spirit, drugs, and glands. We are just now beginning to understand these processes. Perhaps medical science will help us better understand the relation, but our job in the meantime is to avoid unintentional disconnects. Our job is to find out when and how we unintentionally use up too much of our energies in ways that cost us more than we want.

Protecting the Natural

I am not interested in defending or denouncing the use of drugs. I leave that task to those who are still living by a belief that effects are good or bad in themselves. But I am interested in protecting my ability to have a natural inner experience and in avoiding as many as possible of the downs which disconnect me from myself and others.

The danger is not in getting addicted by drinking, taking pills, smoking marijuana, or that smoking will lead to stronger drugs. If addiction is in one's consciousness, one can become addicted to anything from cigarettes to popcorn. There is danger whenever a person believes that any effect is good or that it has power in itself, no matter if it is food, drink, medicine, money, drugs, or anything else.

As I said, everything that we can interpret in third-dimensional terms is at the phenomenal level, is an effect. Food, drink, drugs, and even such esoteric phenomena as ESP and its identifiable results are all effects. They are not the real causes. The real cause is in the spirit of man which leads him to depend on effects. Whenever we become dependent on effects, we may cut ourselves off from the source. The down or problem is not in the effect but in the disconnect we unintentionally bring by depending on the effects. Whenever we use effects, we can ask ourselves: Am I becoming dependent on this effect? If we are, then obviously we are being disconnected from the natural source of our own inner being.

Whenever we believe that any effect is good, we are bringing on a disconnect because we are neglecting the spirit. Actually, I should say that the only "power" is within man. A lot of effects are groovy. They are desirable to have. But in themselves they are neither bad nor good. If we think they are, we are back in the old mind-bound day. And the same applies to drugs. They are neither bad nor good; so we must watch that we don't think they, in themselves, are good any more than we should think they are bad.

When any effect is used in such a way that it keeps us from grooving on life, it is a down. Whenever something is used because we want to avoid a down, we may be cheating ourselves of the value of the down. Whenever an effect is used as means of escaping from the now, it is being misused. When effects come into our lives as a result of the now, when they are a natural part of the present, then they fit into wholeness.

The point is that these principles apply to the use of any effect. Any effect, if it is misused or if we become dependent on it, dissipates the energies of the self. Use effects but don't be used by them.

When people try dangerous stunts just for the fun of it, just for kicks, they are showing that they are not grooving on life. When people use so-called speed or pep pills—amphetamines, Methedrine, Dexedrine, Benzadrine, and other stimulants which accelerate life all out of proportion, they are gobbling up life. For a brief period they may be seeing life from an exciting, jazzed-up view, but they had better get a lot out of it because they are sucking at the substance of life, and in the end they have a corresponding down which might take days to pay for. These stimulants release adrenaline and other energies needed for the future. Tomorrow's energies are being used up today.

The down of using up tomorrow today is that boredom sets in. The person who has used up his tomorrow is disconnected from the ever-constant joy and excitement of life that is at his fingertips when his head is naturally high. He is bored because he has used up the juices which might have oiled the hours.

Each person has the potential of being the full blossom of God on earth. That's why we are here. We are like buds ready to bloom into flowers. Those of us who are here are particularly lucky because this is the spring of humankind. A great mass blooming is now taking place. Perhaps a little fertilizing and pruning can help, but it's all happening. We should encourage the blossom, but it would be foolish to pry the bud open by force.

We can grow to the place where we are able to experience an inner exaltation over a beautiful sunset, where we experience rapture at a work of art or a flower. We need these experiences in order to relate to the spiritual senses within us. We need these experiences before we can understand inner experiences of any kind. Anyone, young or old, who has not had spiritual experience from within himself, in a natural way, must always watch his balance because it may be hazardous for him to mess around with consciousness in areas he has no past experience with which to relate.

The high some people reach with a drug seems to be the ultimate to them because previously they were living in a depressed state which they thought was a normal condition for people. They didn't know the difference. It is fine that such people found that life didn't have to be earthbound, but it would be a disconnect if they then failed to come to the realization that they don't need drugs to be high. It can be a natural state.

A great danger of forcing a high unnaturally is that it is like trying to reach the top without the underpinnings. When Plato said that man was in a cave looking at the shadows on the walls, thinking he was looking at life, he might have added that if man turned suddenly and looked at the sun without being prepared, he could possibly blind himself. Or when Jesus said we must come by the sheepfold and that anyone who came another way was a thief and a robber, he might have meant that looking straight at the sun without being prepared could rob one of achieving the life of light as a natural and permanent experience.

Finally, drugs can present a very real problem in regard to meditation. Through using drugs, many people have attained an appetite for what they could achieve naturally, but the drug experience is so close to meditation that they become confused. The differences between being high through drugs and high through meditation are subtle. One who is familiar with drugs might keep trying to make the natural experience conform to the drug experience. It is sort of like trying to learn Spanish and Italian at the same time. They are so similar that one can get hopelessly confused. It has been my experience that a high on marijuana is like meditating through a screen. It's close, but not the clear uninterrupted contact of the natural high. Also, drugs can even use the spiritual energies needed for meditation in such a way as to make meditation impossible.

Changing Directions

It's one thing to explain how drugs and other effects can bring on disconnects that keep us from meditating or doing other things that we'd like to do, but it's another matter to invent ways to reestablish contact once it has been broken. Our morality isn't complete unless it in-

cludes some basic principles that we can follow in case
we want to change habitual disconnects, large or small.

Of course, the most important and absolute way by
which one can be reestablished and bring on a healing
or change is through spiritual means, which we will
touch on in the next chapters, but there are also ways
the man of earth can set about changing his patterns
through his personal actions.

The (first) and most important, principle is that the
(spirit) in which we are undertaking steps toward accomplishing a change must be up, positive, or high. We
must realize that there is no evil to fight, nothing to
resist. We must be clear that we are not taking action
negatively in order to change some evil, but rather that
we act because we wish to experience some new or creative activity—for positive reasons.

The main reason that most psychiatrists, ministers,
and counselors have not achieved positive results in their
attempts to change people's harmful habits, or sexual
and drug patterns, is because they have been unable to
help people in ways that don't imply the presence of
an evil. They started with the premise or implication
that the habit was bad and needed changing. In condemning the addiction, the therapist had the wrong (spirit,)
or their patient did, and the condemnation just gave
the habit more power. When guilt or condemnation is
present, cures are impossible and the only thing left to
do is to make a kind of prison warden out of the mind
with which the person can try to discipline himself mentally.

It's a matter of self-love. As long as we are trying to change one of our habits, thinking it is evil, we cannot love ourselves and cannot change. When we realize, without condemnation, that we have some habit which causes us to miss out on other things that we would like to experience, we can proceed to try to change the old habit out of the desire to experience something new rather than a desire to fight the old. This is a positive approach in a positive spirit. It's an up, not a down, approach.

Perhaps I am belaboring the point, but we *must* stay in love with ourselves at all times, which means that we must not see ourselves as being evil or separate from God because of some habit or pattern we have. We must not see a habit as a power apart from God. If we do, we are back in the old duality and we will never experience the new.

Say, for instance, that we have found a degree of inner experience by the use of drugs and now we would like to do it natural; we would now like to experience contact with God through meditation. Or perhaps we have known only homosexual relationships and we would like to experience a heterosexual relation. In both cases, we can desire the new experience, believing that it may be a high one, but we must not feel down about our old selves or condemn ourselves for not having been able to experience the natural in the past. The slate must be clean. We must look ahead, not backward. We must go into the new in just the right spirit with our will positive and right, or there is no use trying at all.

Now, because we have known sex or inner experiences

in only one certain way in the past, we have to give ourselves time for that old conditioning to subside. We so greatly identify the experience as happening only one way that we have to give ourselves time to let it come another way. Again, we have to give ourselves time in the right spirit, not grudgingly.

We have to let a certain amount of time pass because we all have need for highs or the right kind of sexual contact, and often we have to give it time to evolve. For instance, in a rather oversimple way, we take ordinary things such as hamburgers or bacon and eggs for granted, but anyone who has traveled abroad knows that after a year out of the country, he would give ten dollars for a real hamburger or some bacon and eggs. So when a person wants to experience a new thing, he has to let himself create the space to make it possible.

If a person who uses drugs wants to have a spiritual experience, he should build up his appetite for a spiritual experience by abstaining from having his extrasensual experiences through drugs. He should not keep his mind filled with thoughts about drugs, and should frequent ten step groups who are trying to do it "natural," for they encourage each others desire to do it natural grow.

You see, the first experience that one has in meditation will probably not be as strong or obvious as the impact of a drug-induced experience, though it can be. One has to really be hungry for that non-phenomenal experience, and then, when it gently starts, one may have to spend months making it grow and get stronger and stronger. It is like an athlete building up muscles over time with constant use and attention.

Finally, however, after we have abstained from the old and placed ourselves in surroundings conducive to the new, the new consciousness takes over and the new experience can ignite. But the new experience will ignite only if the imagination is cooperative. Nothing succeeds, under grace, unless our will is positively directed and our imagination is cooperative. Whenever the will and the imagination are in conflict, the imagination will always win. The forms of our lives are created out of our imagination, so there is no use in kidding ourselves. If we have a negative imaginations, if we condition our imaginations with paranoia or fear, if we have traces of condemnation in our imaginations, we are locked into the old and can't experience or create a shiny new.

On the other hand, we can go anywhere our imaginations can go, we can create anything our imaginations can visualize, and we can experience any joy of life we want—but we can do it only if we are not earthbound, if we are free from the belief in bad and good, and if we love ourselves.

CHAPTER EIGHT

The Meditation Miracle

The mysteries of meditation and the efficacy of prayer
have been dangled before the eyes of mankind, offering
a sort of mystical pot of gold at the end of its spiritual
rainbow, for too long a time. It is true that an inexplicable
alchemy takes place when man experiences contact with
the source within himself, but there is no need now
for all the mumbo jumbo surrounding the attainment
of this mystery. The techniques of how to meditate or
pray have all too often been cloaked in a kind of snobbish
exclusivity designed not only to whet man's appetite
but also to blackmail him into signing away his individuality by joining a particular cult or accepting some one
system over others as the authentic way of going about
meditating.

It is up to us now, in the light of a new morality, to
reveal the art of mediation as a present experience for
all. First, under grace, we must realize that there is no
sin or evil to be overcome as a prelude to the experience
of God. Second, there are some steps we can take, and

if we take them in the right spirit, all the obstacles will dissolve.

In the past, the implication has always been that we must give up everything in order to experience God, that we must reject the material world. Naturally, most people couldn't take that step because deep down inside they knew that the spirit of a true way couldn't include a rejection of life but rather must include an all encompassing love for life.

Obviously, a spiritual approach to meditation puts no one and nothing down. It knows that all mankind is one with God, so every man can realize his oneness. It is not exclusively for a person of one particular sex, nationality, or occupation, in one specific place or time. No fee need be paid, no human initiation is required, no lengthy discipline is demanded; in fact, spiritual contact is, as the Bible tells us, a "gift of God," and gifts are not earned by human effort. If we are not aware that each one of us already has this gift in our hands, it is because mankind has hidden it from us by mind-bending words, so let us find it.

In order to find out the truth of meditation, we must answer a few questions. What actually is spiritual contact? How does it feel? What does it do? Why must we consciously make contact? What do prayer and meditation have to do with this contact? Then, how do we make contact? What are the techniques?

What is spiritual contact? To begin with, it is not all that mysterious. We have all felt it at one time or another to some degree, but often we haven't realized it. We haven't been aware of it, but we actually live by contact; it is our natural state. Since we haven't always consciously realized when we were in contact, we haven't taken conscious recourse to it in order to live life more fully and wholly.

Contact takes place any time we have ceased to be alone and cut off from the source of life, when our own separate personal vibration has been dropped and we step into rhythm with the vibration of life itself. Any time we are healed or recharged, strengthened or supplied, we are in contact.

How does it feel? It feels like being mentally, physically, and spiritually washed. It feels like exaltation. It feels like the bubbling up of joy within. It feels like being free of bodily limitations. That is why I say we all feel contact every time we experience delight over a work of art, a job well done, or a sport well played, or when we feel appreciation for man's accomplishments. We feel it every time we sense that we belong. That's why human beings have such a desire to belong—it is hunger for the spiritual experience of oneness. Contact is the feeling of being recharged. It is the feeling of desireless love just for the sake of love itself. It is the feeling of light. It is the feeling of not only hearing a song but also being the song. It is spiritual goose pimples.

What does it do? It cleans us. It reestablishes us when we are cut off. It chases away the cobwebs of the mind and spirit. It reveals to us where we have mistakenly got off the track. It heals us. It frees us to love. It makes us one with the universe. All of that and vastly more.

Why must we consciously make contact if we are actually in contact all the time? We are in the morning of the day of grace when nothing need be rejected or put down. In order to live this new life, a conscious attainment of the contact experience is a necessity in order for us to live by guidelines which are not judgmental. In the old day, under law, people didn't realize the importance of making conscious contact with their true selves. They let their minds live them; they set rules which were to apply day after day, telling them what was bad and what was good so they would know how to act and react. All people had to do was to follow the laws. Now, under grace, we know there is nothing on the face of creation which is always bad or always good. At each moment we must have some way of checking in with the truth in order to see if a person, place, or thing is in its right place, doing what it is "for." Making contact is how we check in. It is the way the third-dimensional man of earth checks in with his own fourth-dimensional man of God self. That check-in may take only a second, but it reveals the truth of life to such an extent that earth man can live for hours in a harmony with his material sense of life.

At a certain point the mind lets go and a oneness with all of life is felt. We are never quite the same after we have experienced this conscious contact or the inrush of energy and life. We still have to face all kinds of earthly problems, but never again are they quite the same—neither we nor the problems.

I have traveled a great deal, and for a number of years

I thought I could imagine what it was like to go around the whole world. I had touched so many places in my sorties out from this country and back that I thought by simply piecing together all of my impressions, I would know what a full trip would be like. Once I finally made it all the way around the world in one trip, I felt surprisingly different. Now, instead of my being in the world, the world was in *me*. I held it complete within my consciousness. Once we have had a conscious experience in meditation which transcends our finite sense of self, we know what it feels like not to be in ourselves but to contain ourselves within ourselves.

Prayer and Meditation

Prayer and meditation are not the actual contact. They are just our will or intent directed toward the contact. As such, they are really part of the third-dimensional sense of life. They, in themselves, are not spiritual but are part of humanhood. They are part of our imagination in its attempt to create a contact through imaging it; they are a necessary step that the man of earth must take in order to arrive at the point of contact.

It is rather like a Boy Scout trying to make fire. He has to have a piece of flint and a piece of metal. He must keep them clean, dry, and in good condition if he expects to make fire. He hits the two together, maybe many times, in order to get the spark. The spark is the miracle, the contact. It is the flash point. Though it happens in the twinkling of an eye, it can start a whole fire.

Prayer and meditation are our tools. Prayer is mainly the intent or spirit in which we set out to make contact, and meditation is mainly the technique or physical means against which the intent is struck. When the two are in good shape, the contact is made and the fire of life is lighted.

Prayer is commonly associated with the Occident and Hebrew-Christianity; so is the love of materiality and the world. Symbolic or otherwise, the word made flesh, or the importance of raising material standards, has always been more strongly emphasized in the West. Westerners' intent and their prayers have been directed toward personal and physical freedom. Their mistake has been in getting a sense of right and wrong mixed in with their intent, but at least Westerners haven't rejected the world. The Orient has seen the danger in trying to make the world conform to man's ideas of bad and good; so the Orient has perfected meditation as the technique for dropping the personal sense and merging with God, but this in turn has often become a rejection of the world.

Now, however, we are in the new day when we realize we reach the fourth dimension both by merging so deeply in action that we become one with life and by refraining at other times from taking action. Prayer is spiritually directed action, and meditation is spiritual cessation from action. Both are necessary.

In the Western world, we have distorted the right idea of prayer. We go to God asking for material things or for God to do our will, and instead of getting what we really want, we accomplish the opposite. We image duality and we create it. Anything we acknowledge, we demonstrate. In that respect, prayer is *acknowledgement* and vice versa. Even our *opinions are prayers* in that they create the flow of our imagination and intent.

We quite naturally want harmony, and we know that it will be reestablished if we make contact, but the paradox is that we must go into prayer or meditation wanting *contact*, not *things*. The right kind of prayer intent is to meditate in an effort to find ourselves, not to get something for ourselves.

Prayer is a kind of knocking at the door of the collective unconscious. We have been so in the habit of taking thought in order to live our lives that we find we must change the direction. Prayer or contemplation is the act of changing the habit of *thinking* into the habit of *listening*. It is possible to listen to the still small voice within, to listen for a feeling. At any rate, prayer certainly isn't prayer unless it achieves a state beyond the thinking mind. Rather than taking thought, prayer is the process of freeing the mind. It means dropping all conditioned thought. It is *centering*—centering one's being in wholeness, not leaving it top-heavy in the mind.

Prayer is a kind of dying. Dying to the mind. As such, it is not a thing but a condition. It makes no difference how you get to that condition, but when you have let go of the sense of personal power, you have prayed.

When I was working with John van Druten, the playwright, on *I Am A Camera*, the play that was turned into the musical, *Cabaret*, he would call me in whenever he got stuck, and we would discuss the problem. Sometimes we could solve the problem by using our intelligence, but at other times we were unable to find an answer. One day a particularly difficult enigma was presented to us. After lengthy discussion, we gave up. We prayed; it was our intent to find help through prayer. Before long we both became aware of, "I of my own self can do nothing." Boom, the answer to our problem came through.

The next day another problem came in the course of the writing. Again I went to John's office and we discussed the situation awhile. When no answer came, we said, "All right, let's pray." Both of us thought we knew "how" to do it. We said, "I of my own self can do nothing." Then again, "I of my own self can do nothing." And again, "I of my own self can do nothing." And that's what we got—nothing. Finally in desperation we gave up, feeling that it didn't work anymore—and then boom, once more the answer came through. The point is, subconsciously we thought that by thinking, "I of my own self can do nothing," we were creating the vacuum or getting out of our way, but we weren't. We were still thinking that there actually was something we could do. However, when we panicked and once more let go, we arrived again at that open state where we could listen—could pray.

Listening is the key to prayer. It is the place where truth leaves the intellectual mind of reason and enters the soul where it is experienced.

This shifting makes a kind of spiritual change of chemistry in a person. Actually, the change affects even our material bodies. In the transition from larva to butterfly, the worm attaches itself to a limb, weaves a cocoon around itself, goes into a kind of meditative state, and changes its chemistry, resulting in a totally new body which emerges as a butterfly. Perhaps one day scientists will discover how that same glandular action is brought on by prayer or meditation, altering our physical condition. Even if they do, I doubt that they will be able to explain how man can bring on this change purely from within himself.

The ability to bring on this change within ourselves is a new definition for *maturity*. A person is spiritually mature if and when they know how to pray.

After all, maturity is gauged by our ability to handle the pressures, the emergencies, and the problems we face in an unemotional and constructive fashion. We can't do that unless we have found some way of keeping in touch with our oneness. No matter how we accomplish keeping inner contact, that way is prayer, because prayer is the ability to anchor within and withstand negative or confusing vibrations. Prayer is one thing—our attempt to experience our God self.

This kind of maturity has nothing to do with our age or type. When we do not react to upsetting or frustrating conditions, we are mature. Our ability to perform in a mature fashion shows we are able to make contact with God.

Techniques of Meditation

Don't believe anyone who says he knows how to meditate. It is possible to individually find techniques which aid us in arriving at the flash point, but there isn't a successful meditation in which the person doesn't come to the point of giving up, of realizing he doesn't really know how to make it happen. When that point of human impossibility arrives, contact takes place. As long as we think we have the power to make it happen, we are still operating under the human mind and it doesn't happen. Ask anyone who has achieved the contact and he will admit that each time he experiences contact he feels for one split second that he is not going to get there this time, that he is helpless.

Our vibration or state of consciousness when we attempt to meditate may not be the same as the last time we meditated, so we must find different techniques to help us at different times. There is no one way.

Once, when I was on a television program in California, the interviewer asked me, "How do you meditate or pray?" My answer sounded rather flippant at first. I replied, "Which me are you talking about?" I went on to explain that if someone woke me up at the crack of dawn, he might be met at the door by a rather disgruntled me, but if he knocked a couple of hours later, after I had got myself in running order, he would encounter a friendlier person. In the course of a single day, I am operating at a number of different vibrations. I must admit that now I operate at a higher level more of the time than I once did, but nevertheless, my level is not always the same.

Well, I have found for myself that I need different techniques at different times, depending on where I am at the moment. At times, I am so greatly out of contact that I can't get any help from reading or from contemplating. I practically have to return to the old fashioned prayers of my childhood religion, which taught me to get down on by bony knees and call on a God apart from myself. At times I must sort of blank out, take a nap, in order to release my fears. Then, when I wake up, I can start to read spiritual writings or practice other helps until I get my contact going.

At times I must go out into nature, walk by the water, or climb a mountain to make contact. Sometimes people are my prayer. If I communicate with my fellow man I can make contact. And certainly there are times when a kiss from a loved one is a prayer.

Also, at times I am living in such a sense of oneness that it would be not only redundant but also a denial to sit down and meditate. It is there. I need only to look over my shoulder, so to speak, and wink at it. If I were to deny it by thinking I had to become involved in some complicated ritual, I would be turning my back on the fact that IT IS.

To rely entirely on a system anyone else has devised might help for a time, but it does not include the freedom of infinite individuality. Using a ready-made system is rather like using an automatic camera. Today we have cameras on the market which eliminate all of the old hazards of photography. With them, just about anyone can take a good picture. Automatic cameras certainly improve the quality or results for someone who has limited talent, but in turn, these cameras limit one's true freedom. Automatic cameras are set up for the largest averages. In other words, most pictures are taken under certain light conditions so the readings are calibrated for those. Most pictures are taken at medium contrast. To be really free, a photographer has to know how to make his own settings and adjust for pictures taken at any hour or condition. The same applies to meditation. There is no set formula, no technique that fits for everyone at all times.

Before we go into specific aids, I would like to touch on some of the blocks or difficulties that most of us have felt in our attempts at meditation, particularly in our early days. At the beginning, we are often faced with the most primary kinds of self-consciousness. Our minds do everything they can to keep us from relaxing into meditation. If other people are around, we feel personally embarrassed.

I remember the first time I tried to meditate in a group. We all closed our eyes and sat silently. The idea felt so preposterous to me that I had a difficult time keeping from giggling, my mind's way of keeping me self-conscious. After I got over that particular temptation it never happened again, but I found that physical discomfort became a great handicap. The minute I tried to get quiet, my body became a beehive of feelings. I was aware of every bone and muscle. If I tried to force stillness on myself, I only managed to spend all my time thinking about my body.

The next trick my mind played on me was to bring on a tremendous desire to go to sleep. Sitting there with my eyes closed I would find myself dozing off, and though

I had every desire to go beyond my sense of self, I could do no more than concentrate on staying awake. Actually that was a good state because it always preceded a triumph over the mind. After the desire to sleep passed, my mind became fully alive, not with thoughts but with listening from within. Sometimes it was best to take a little nap rather than fight the mind by trying to stay awake. After the nap, my mind was quiet and contact was more easily attained.

There are also a few mental annoyances. The first is the belief that you don't have enough understanding to meditate. That, too, is a trick. You don't need understanding; you just need the desire or intent. The rest is up to God, or the truth of one's self.

After you have experienced a bit in meditation, you may have psychic visions or experiences. They take over the mind by making you believe that it is necessary to have these experiences or that you haven't made contact without them. That isn't true. You might very well hear sounds, see lights, or experience a number of manifestations, but those things are no more than signposts on the road. If you are tricked into believing that signs are necessary, you have forgotten the trip for the scenery.

Perhaps more people have been led astray by psychic phenomena than any other single thing. After an experience which manifests itself in some phenomenon, they proceed to become more involved in the phenomenon than in the contact. Look at the word phenomenon." It tells the story. Anything to do with psychic phenomena which is explainable is of the phenomenal world. That makes it not a spiritual thing, but a phenomenal one.

I'm not putting down psychic phenomena, spiritualism, prophecy, or any of the other events usually associated with spiritual realization. I am just saying that they are not spiritual, as such; they are humanly identifiable and part of the third dimension. Perhaps they are a high form of the human, but they are human representations nevertheless, and if you get them confused with pure contact or the fourth dimension, you may find your meditations blocked and contact lost. You may find yourself back in the mental way of life.

If you experience voices, colors, or sounds, you can note the fact, you can appreciate that your contact produced the experience, but if you want to keep the intent of meditation pure, you must keep it focused on the experience of God, not psychic phenomena.

By the same token, you might find that after you start meditating, your physical system wants purer food or simpler eating habits. Perhaps you don't want to eat meat anymore. That is fine, but if your mind tricks you into believing that there is virtue in being a vegetarian, or that eating meat has power over you, you are once more operating at the third-dimensional level of phenomena.

The greatest mental block to the experience has been perpetrated in the name of meditation itself. Because certain practitioners of meditation haven't realize that there is no evil, nothing to be condemned, and because they have no yardstick or morality of grace to measure with, their systems of meditation are based on the belief that there is a material world one has to overcome. They teach that we start in the gross world or the gross sense of life, then rise to the fine or subtle sense which goes beyond our limited sensual understanding, and finally we can experience the spiritual. In a way this is right, because we do go from our physical to a higher, super but not superior, sense, but as long as we label the physical as being gross or evil or less good, we are back in the old duality. As long as we see the world as gross, we are dropping out from being fully human. Any system of meditation which is based on the premise that the natural is gross is condemning the world and isn't a spiritual approach—the spirit is wrong.

Those who experience some of the subtle sensual levels for the first time are discovering a whole new world, and they can easily think it is the spiritual world. But actually it is a subtle material expansion. Those who, in the same way, experience the subtle world through LSD or some other mind-altering agent might easily think they have discovered the spiritual world. In fact, they have experienced an extension of the material world rather than the spiritual.

Then, too, a number of teachings, under the guise of meditation, say that we must use the mind to experience the subtle world until the mind arrives at the transcendent. But the danger is that the mind stays in control, and the real experience eludes us.

All of those teachings which advocate definite systems,

which advocate disciplining the mind as though it is an enemy, which reject any activity or material thing, are still in the old day. They were right for their time and we can learn from them, but in this new day, we are our own teachers and we devise our own systems which work for us individually.

Some ABC's of Meditation

Meditation is like altering the direction of a wheel. It is shifting from the man of earth to the man of God self. We must first slow the wheel down, then stop it, and then start it rolling the other direction. For what we might call silent or formal meditation, in which we attempt to make contact and to commune by sitting quietly, turned within, there are some tips which might help. First, we slow the body down, then the mind and the senses.

In order to slow the body down and have the maximum control over it, sitting has always been considered the number one requirement for students of Zen and the oriental religions which specialize in meditation. In the cross-legged sitting position which is called the lotus position, the body is rested yet the spine is straight; the nervous system is not pinched but is at its maximum to freedom.

Sitting on the floor isn't necessary, however. We in the West are not trained to sit cross-legged, so if we prefer we can sit in a chair which allows body freedom. The best chair is probably one with a straight back which keeps us from hunching or unequally distributing our body weight and allows us to rest our feet comfortably on the floor. It may be padded or at least not too hard and irregular. We can each try out various types of chairs until we find one in which we feel most comfortable and least aware of our bodies.

The belief that we absolutely must have a guru or teacher is also part of the old day. Most of us can find help from a teacher. Most often our fire is lighted from a teacher's fire, but, in fact, our consciousness is what has led us to the teacher in the first place. Our teacher is a creation of our own oneness with God, the God within our own being, only it is expressed outwardly as our teacher. If we believe that having a teacher is an absolute necessity, we have forgotten that we are in the new day when our oneness with God constitutes our oneness with all being. Our oneness with universal being is our true guru or teacher. A human teacher can only show us the aids he has found, but infinity can reveal helps which no single teacher knows.

It is a good idea to find a special quiet place for meditation in our homes. If we retreat day after day to some chair or corner in order to meditate, we find after a while that the place creates a kind of vibration or aura which helps us become quiet.

After sitting down in order to meditate, our first goal is, as the orientals say, to *one-point* our minds and senses. That means we want to slow down the flow of thoughts and senses, create a kind of vacuum so that the spirit can be felt.

Perhaps we have found that we are helped in our

infinity of being if we create a kind of altar. This isn't necessary—in fact, it is harmful if we get superstitious about it—but it can be useful if our intent is not distorted. As we are making the voyage from the material sense to the spiritual sense, we may like to put a flower on our altar as the recognition of God's beauty expressed through nature. Perhaps we want to light a candle or incense. Actually, all of those things can have a dual purpose. They are dedications, and yet they are aids to one-pointing our senses.

We can even concentrate on the candle flame or the flower, or smell the incense, and in so doing, our whole being, body, mind, and spirit, is set about the task of letting go.

It is harder but even more necessary to one-point the mind than the senses, and there are several ways we find help in that. Sometimes we can read from illumined writings which attract us, perhaps the Bible or the Gita, until we feel an answering response within us. When we do, it is advisable to close the book and try to hold the feeling, not the thought, that the reading brought on. When the feeling slips away, we can open the book and repeat the experience. This reading and feeling can act like the starter on a motorboat. We try it and try it, and all of a sudden the motor sputters and starts. Then we don't need the book anymore; we are hearing from within. *Voice of The Silence*

Above all, we should not fight our thoughts in our attempts at meditation. Such struggling is like resisting evil; it only creates more thought. Thoughts don't really have power to keep us away from the contact. Just love them. Give them wings, and they will fly away. Without fighting, we can gently bring our mind back to the center, to the aim of our activity.

Frequently people say, "I can't meditate because I can't stop thinking." But thoughts don't have power. Thinking isn't the problem. The problem is when we think thinking is a handicap and try to resist thinking as though it is an evil. The spirit of resistance is what gets in our way.

Though we don't fight the mind, there are some helps we can use in returning the mind to center. One of these is the Hindu technique of the use of the mantra. A mantra is a word or phrase on which we can concentrate in order to bring ourselves into line with the vibration of being. The Christian religion contains many mantralike statements, such as, "Thy grace is sufficient for me in all things," or, "I have come that ye might be fulfilled," or even the Hail Mary of the Catholic Church. When we find our mind wandering, we can gently direct it by returning to a contemplation of our mantra.

Above all, we are not trying to bludgeon the mind out of existence. We want to blank the mind so it can be used by the spirit, but we want it to be alive and free.

In the past a teacher gave his student a mantra designed for the student's present state of consciousness. The idea was that when the student reached a higher state, a more advanced mantra would be given to him. Initiation only meant that the guru meditated with the student, sensed what vibration the student was experiencing, and gave him a mantra to fit. If the student was in a very personal or restless vibration, his mantra would fit that situation.

Often a beginning student was told to meditate on some simple word like "peace" to slow down his fears. When that had been attained he was told to meditate on "not this, not this, but thou, thou," as a way of shifting from the human sense to God identification. Eventually he would be ready to meditate on "I am and God is." Often a student was told to meditate on a word without real or human meaning in order to lift the mind beyond conditioned thought—as the word "OM" is used by the Hindu, and "IS" is used by the occidental.

Is, just is or isness, has nothing the mind can hang on to, so it is easy to go beyond thought to feeling. Everyone needs such an indefinable word at one time or another.

Finally, we can arrive at the absolute. We can contemplate the word "I," the pure oneness within. But at that time we should have reached the state where the *I-ness* is comprehended without its being mixed up with personal identification.

As I said before, we go to meditation at different times in different states on consciousness; no single mantra is always the right one. It is up to us, under our new morality, to sense what state of awareness we are in and use whatever mantra works for us at that time. If we get quiet and listen, our spirit will tell us our mantra.

In place of one set mantra we can begin by contemplating whatever truths come into our mind. Perhaps Bible quotations will pop to our attention. If we mull them, listen to them, contemplate them, we may begin to feel a sense of silence within or we may find light flooding our being. One quote may flow into another, and another, until we realize that it isn't our mind bringing them forth, but rather that they come from the collective unconscious, or God. Don't forget, man's words mean little, but God's words are powerful and sharp as a sword. God's words can move the world, and they slip into contemplation before we know it. But they do it in silence, the silence within. Contemplation can be a help, but only if it leads to silence.

Finally, after we have yielded our bodies, after we have stilled our senses, after we have concentrated our minds so intensely as to recede from externals into emotional stillness, after we have contemplated truth until we reach silence, we experience the flash point. Perhaps we feel an inner click, a deep sigh that goes right to our toes, perhaps an inner sense of light, even a bubbling up of joy. It takes only a split second. It is seldom more than the most brief of moments. But in that moment, God is on the field and we are merged into life itself. We feel serenity and exaltation of body and spirit.

When, Where, and After Contact

Once we have recognized contact with God in our meditation, everything else falls into place. After making contact, we can take those problems we have put aside—in order to keep from going into meditation with human desires—and hold them up to the light of our inner contact. Now we can let our minds drift across our life like a radar over a radar scope. When a person, place, or thing pops into our consciousness, we measure it against the release we have just had and receive the guidance we can be given from within. We don't hoard the experience; we don't drop out by trying to keep on perpetuating the feeling indefinitely.

Even here some people have lost the way. They have experienced the joy of a contact in meditation but believed that there was some virtue in long meditations. There isn't. Overlong meditation sessions are even self-indulgent. They are similar to getting "stoned" by taking too many drugs.

The object of meditation is to receive the light and then come back into the world to make it a more light-filled place. I know it is tempting to want to stay in that peace; it is often hard to return to the active world. But meditation for the sake of personal enjoyment alone is a disconnect with the world and our responsibility to our fellow man. It is far better to make the contact many times in a day than to sit for long times in one stretch.

There are special times for meditation, but any time is the right time. For my money, the most important time is at the beginning of each day in order to get programmed for the day, to get the right vibration started. The second most important time to meditate is before going to bed at night. An evening meditation sort of flushes out the day, rejects the unintentional irritants one has taken on by third-dimensional living. Then the night is more restful and we find we even need less sleep. But any time is the right time.

During the course of a day, we may feel what I call pulls or pressures. These are signs to us that we need to get in step. Most of us know that if we get started on the wrong foot we may stay out of step until we change our vibration. Meditation is how we do it.

Even if we are off in the business world, when we feel a pull or heaviness we can always find a private corner or close our office door for a moment of meditation. When we don't feel a pull or pressure, there is probably no need at the moment to meditate unless we wish to renew the contact for the sheer joy of it.

The time it takes for meditation varies. Sometimes it happens in a moment. It may take an hour to make the contact. There is no law. Each must come to know his or her self. Each must come to know what it feels like to contact God as personally as he or she knows what it feels like to contact the one they love.

CHAPTER NINE

The Healing Spirit

The subject of healing has been the hot potato of the Christian message, or any spiritual message, for that matter. It can't be ignored, and yet no one has known how to handle it. After the early years of Christianity, when the Christian message was codified and placed under law, the spirit of grace departed, and with it went the ability to heal. The secrets of healing were still buried in the Christ message, but man was blinded to them. From then on healing became a cruel subject. On one hand, healing was held out as a possibility which was bound up in the spiritual life. On the other hand, people's hopes were constantly dashed to the ground by man's inability to bring healing about.

In the past few years, the possibility of spiritual healing has been brought out again because we have arrived at the spiritual day, and healing is an integral part of the life lived by grace. But even now there is a great deal of confusion about healing, for this is a time of transition.

Most reasonable people shy away from the whole subject of spiritual healing. I did. I had come from a family of physicians. The doctors in my family were sometimes called in too late to save the failures of those who tried to force healings with their minds or blind faith but didn't know what they were doing. Naturally, my physician family thought spiritual healers were the devil's handmaids.

I also wanted desperately to rise beyond having to judge the world in terms of bad or good, sick or well. I wanted to love the world, not judge it, not say, "O.K., I'll love you when you are better, more healthy, more wealthy, more successful."

I couldn't stomach any more personal guilt, and if I had to consider sickness as failure and health as success, then I would be back in the old trap of not being able to love myself whenever I was sick.

Most important of all, I felt I had to believe in God in order to have an inner anchor, but I was too intelligent to believe that God could be God if there were any other power apart from God. If I equated God with healing, I would have to believe that either God failed where sickness was concerned or else God was some kind of a monster who allowed sickness to take place unless people said the right words or thought the right thoughts.

The whole subject smelled of hypocrisy, of man's ego, of wishful thinking, of blind faith, of people's disappointments which in turn made them lose faith in the true source within themselves. I wanted none of it. So when I came into a growing awareness of what it meant to live by spirit, I rather resented the intrusion of the subject of healing. I didn't want to cloud up the water. Then, little by little, I couldn't help but notice how my own health began to improve as I progressed on my search. Sometimes patterns of ill health were mysteriously replaced by illogically quick recovery. Other illnesses left without the help of medication. I wasn't just healed physically. All kinds of personal problems involving a need for money and human relations seemed to dissolve as a result of some kind of spiritual influence. I had to face the reality of spiritual healing. And with this, I had to face my own responsibility toward healing both myself and others.

Nobody in their right mind wants to set himself up as a healer. First of all, nobody knows how to heal. Even a doctor knows that he can prescribe medication but he can't actually produce healing, any more than a mother can raise a fingernail on her child. The healing process may operate by using a person as an instrument, but none of us knows any more how to heal than we do how to meditate or to know God.

Besides being an impossibility, healing also presents a personal danger. Any time someone sets himself up as either a healer or a spiritual teacher, he puts himself in a position where eventually he assumes a kind of personal superiority—he implies that he has the message the public needs, or that he has the power to help God out. Unless those who proclaim themselves as healers are very solidly anchored in spirit, before long they begin to believe that they have power themselves.

The desire to heal or teach tempts one to forget that

the kingdom of heaven is already here. The temptation
to change the world is a put-down of the world. When
a person begins to think of himself as a healer, he begins
to cut himself off from the source. Little by little his
effectiveness decreases. Healing is effective because of
someone's capacity to break the illusion of separateness
by experiencing that there actually is no evil to fight.
If that person calls himself a healer he has to live up to
the title, so an unsuccessful healer has to start compromis-
ing, falling back on law, finding an excuse, and blaming
others for his failure. It's a title to avoid.

But, and this is an important *but* to understand, the
higher we go in consciousness, the more we experience
our own oneness, the more others are attracted to us
for help. Others sense a vibration—a harmonizing, cleansing, or healing vibration. Most often those who come
around a person who has achieved some awareness of
the life lived by grace don't even know what they come
for; they just know they want to be near that person.
Often they start asking for help in little indirect ways.
They may not say, "Pray for me," or "Heal me," but
they say, "I feel better after I have been with you," "I
get a lift from you," "There's something about you that
helps me and makes my problems go away"—and that's
the same as asking for help.

Then it is the response-ability of the person who has
the lifted consciousness to give help, for giving help is
giving self. One has to for purely selfish reasons: one
has to in order to be alive and living. He or she has to
give in order to be blessed with the life force which

makes them spiritually attractive to others. But mostly, the person who has the capacity to bring on healings has to lift and heal others because he knows that everyone is connected to him; everyone is a projection of his own inner self; everyone has come into his consciousness and are therefore a part of himself just as his own hands and feet are connected to his body.

Even those to whom no one is turning for help must start healing. After all, we get by our giving. If we wish to be made whole ourselves, we have to start making others whole. We can begin in the simplest of ways. We don't even need to let anyone know, but every time an appearance of inharmony or disconnect appears in the lives of those around us, we can begin by seeing through the appearance to the truth.

Finally, however, and this sounds as if I am contradicting my statement that no one should set himself or herself up as a healer, we must make a commitment to others by letting them know we are willing to do what we can. We don't have to say, "I will heal you," in a manner which mistakes the *I* for the ego, but we must let our family of mankind know that we are all linked together and that we are ready to offer our consciousness at any time it is wanted.

It is easy just to say, "I'll pray for you." But if the word "pray" is too sticky with the sound of old morality, we can say, "Anytime you want to use some of my up, my contact, my juice, it is yours." That's saying, "I'll pray for you." Anytime we let others know we are going to go off somewhere quiet and release their problems for them—which is easier for us to do than it is for them because they are more personally involved—we are saying, "I will pray for you." When we get over judging and can experience inner harmony, we are praying for them, we are healing them.

Now, this has nothing to do with one person's being more spiritual than the other. It doesn't mean one person knows more about healing than another. There isn't a person who has read this book, or any of the New Testament for that matter, who doesn't know enough to heal.

It's this: Perhaps one day I am down and you are not. I can say to you, "Give me a zap." And you can, because you are up at that moment. My asking constitutes a link. On another day, you might be down and I am not; so you say to me, "Say, I'm wrecked today, give me some help." And this time I help the healing along.

Meditation and healing go hand in hand. When we meditate and make contact, invariably more wholeness manifests itself. We might say that meditation is *how* and healing is *what*. The paradox is that we cannot meditate with any purpose in mind other than the purpose of letting go and experiencing the allness of life. However, when that allness is experienced in its absolute fourth-dimensional sense, we become more free and whole at the third-dimensional personal level.

When we feel a pull, a down vibration, we recognize it as the signal to go reestablish our wholeness by checking in with our God self. In other words, we know it's time to heal ourselves, and when we heal ourselves, we are contributing to the healing of all others. As a matter of fact, when we feel a pull, it can be for one of three reasons. Something of a purely personal disturbance or "down" is looming on our own horizon. Someone in our family to whom we are hooked up is having a negative experience, which we sense by our oneness with them. Something of a universal nature is affecting the whole family of mankind.

No matter which situation has caused the pull, there is one basic thing we have to do—go back to center and reestablish contact with the truth of being. If we go beyond the temptation to believe in bad and good, realize God is the only power, and free ourselves of any judgment, grace begins to manifest itself once more. We have removed ourselves from law. Wholeness and freedom are established. A healing has taken place.

Alas, the next time a pull comes, or the next time we are presented with a problem, we know that healing can take place, so it is all the more difficult to keep from trying to judge. It's hard to keep from thinking, "That situation is bad—I had better heal it." But when we want to change appearances, we have slipped back into the old way of living where we judged by bad and good. It's tricky.

Sure, healing is a tricky business. But we are safe as long as we remember one thing, as long as we keep this one thought indelibly printed on our foreheads: NO MAN CAN HEAL. The only thing that heals is the breakthrough from the third dimension to an experience of the fourth dimension. The only thing that brings harmony is the ray of light that is let in when a consciousness rises to that level, and no man can do that out of personal will or human knowledge, out of personal power or desire. So remember, "I can't heal anything." And then go heal.

Pitfalls

It is up to us to get clear on just what spiritual healing is in order to avoid the pitfalls. Healing means a reestablishing, returning to wholeness, harmonizing, and fulfilling. It doesn't have to be just a physical healing. Anytime we return to wholeness in supplying our material needs, our creative needs, or in making our human relations whole, we are healing.

The words *heal*, *whole*, and *holy* all come from the same root, an Old English word *hel*, meaning *complete*. When we heal, we make whole, and a whole man is a holy man. Obviously a holy man is one who is operating in complete balance between his earth self and his God self. A holy man is one who has neither dropped out of the world nor turned his back on the material world.

How do we judge holiness in the new day? Simple. We don't! Nothing is holy, and nothing is unholy. Everything we see with our eyes is a finite third-dimensional view, no matter how favorable or unfavorable it appears. Absolutely everything is reaching out to holiness, to becoming more infinite and whole, but no thing and no one seen in terms of the third dimension is holy, whole, or completely healthy. It is up to us to *experience* holiness, not look for it with our eyes and minds.

We don't try to make third-dimensional man holy or whole. We don't try to change anything we see at the phenomenal level. We don't try to bring God into the third-dimensional level; we take man up to God. We recognize the problem, but then we put it aside and experience the universal oneness. As long as we are making treatments or trying to know truths about a person, place, or thing, we are at the mental level and not at the spiritual.

The greatest handicap to spiritual healing is man's good intentions. The more man wants to heal and the more he believes in bad and good, the more tightly he locks himself under law. God already is, perfection already is, wholeness already is. Our job is to experience it, not try to make it true.

We need know only two things in order to heal. One, *that* God is—that there is a ground of all being, a universal wholeness, an ultimate truth, and that all living being is contained in that all-embracing isness. Two, *what* God is—one power against which all beliefs in evil or separateness disappear. That's all we need to know with our minds. The trick is the experiencing of it, but if it is experienced, then discord gives way to harmony and suddenly what appeared destructive is revealed as part of growth, or it just plain dissolves.

One of the saddest things I have witnessed has been churches or groups who were conducting healing services in which, instead of healing, people were doing the exact opposite. No matter how conscientious and well intended the participants were, by not knowing what they were about, they were making matters more difficult. Rather than dissolving the negative into oneness, they were trying to evoke some power over the negative and were instead giving it power. By seeing the people they were trying to help as sick and unfortunate people, the healers were believing in the finite interpretations of the people they wanted to help and were not establishing them in their true identity as one with God.

Sometimes prayer groups use a system in which the members one after another say the name of someone they want the group to pray for. That could be all right if the member didn't say what the claim or down was. When someone says, "Pray for Mary who is having a difficult pregnancy," or, "Pray for John who is in trouble with drugs," they succeed only in causing everyone in the room to visualize a Mary with a difficult pregnancy or a John who can be harmed by drugs. If anything helps create the situation, it is the imagings of those in the room. In turn, if the names alone are voiced without the problem being stated, those who want to heal don't set their imaginations to work creating the problem. Without visualizing the problem, the group thinks, "That person is no different from any of us. We are all whole and one in our spiritual identity." If the group then releases the problem, not to a blind God but to the truth, an experience takes place. The vibration is lifted and the person being prayed for is freed from the problem.

Most of those practices called spiritual healings are not really spiritual; they are mental. We can test whether a practice is mental or spiritual by seeing if it includes taking a human ill or discomfort into the meditation or thought, if it implies that health is better than ill health.

As long as a healing technique implies that the sick person has to do something in order to be healed—for example, they have to think good thoughts, reform, or stop sinning—the would-be healer is dealing from the moral level and is not tuning in to the spiritual level. All the ills one has are like masks one wears at a party. There are hundreds of different masks: the mask of sickness, the mask of poverty, the mask of divorce, the mask of failure. But they all cover one face. That face is a belief in a power apart from God. A spiritual healer knows that the masks are only visible projections of the one problem: a sense of separation from God. He doesn't try to fight the masks. He sees them, then he goes beyond them to the cause. Any teaching that says it is necessary to label the masks is in the mental and not the spiritual.

A spiritual healer deals with a misapprehension of reality, not colds, cancers, drug addiction, stealing, cruelty, or war. A spiritual healer doesn't try to erase the snakes from the wall when a man is undergoing d.t.'s, he doesn't try to fight the goblins that appear in a nightmare. Rather, he sobers up the person and wakes him from the dream. When awake, the previously sick person is whole once more.

Practical Steps

An Episcopalian minister friend and I were talking about healing. He told me how he was called by one of his church families to go sit at the bedside of a man who was dying in the hospital. As he sat there alone in the room beside the man who was in a coma, he tried to pray, as the family had requested. He was overwhelmed with his helplessness and the realization that there wasn't any way he could make God work. In his anguish, he experienced, "I of my own self can do nothing," and to his amazement, before long the patient came out of his coma and in a few days was well. My friend was confused because he didn't know how it had happened. He wasn't aware that by coming to the realization that nothing could be done third-dimensionally, he was lifted beyond bad and good into the spirit, and when the ray of light broke into this level, a healing took place. Actually, he had stopped thinking about the man and had healed himself.

The first step in a practical approach to being an instrument for healing is to realize that we really only heal ourselves. When we heal ourselves of a belief in a power apart from God, the picture we have in our own consciousness changes.

When a person has asked for help, that is all he or she needs to do, and that is all we need from them. They have entered our consciousness by their request for help. It sounds odd, but our job is to realize that the person doesn't need help. Strangely enough, as with good intentions, the best healers are those who seem the most impersonal, who react least to negative appearances. Perhaps this isn't really strange. Look at the strongest person you know, the one to whom you turn for help in a time of trouble, and you will invariably see that he or she is a person who won't react violently or emotionally when you tell them your problem. Such persons are healers. They realize God is still on the field, no matter what appearances testify.

Under grace, the degree of a person's faith is not what they say they believe; it is the degree to which they react.

For instance, one man is told his house is on fire. He immediately goes into a panic, starts running around frantically calling for help. You know by his actions that he is not very secure within, that he thinks his good is bound up in his house, that he doesn't believe in his power to make another house if that one burns.

Another man is told his house is on fire. He almost jokingly says, "Well, let's see what we can do about it. If we can't put it out, maybe we can roast some marshmallows." You know that this man does not base his life on externals, that he isn't disconnected from the source of life.

Now, what do we do if someone telephones us for help? First, we let him tell us the trouble he is in so he can get it off his chest and believe that help is on the way. But it would actually be better if he said no more than "I need help." We know that no matter what the problem is, it is just a belief in a power of evil, so what we are curing is the belief. If we do let someone tell us the problem, we let them tell it only once and not repeat themselves over and over, for that just deepens the problem. We should limit the telephone call as much as possible so we can immediately get our own release. We assure the caller, "I'll be with you," and then get off the line.

It is often best to keep contact by telling the person

to call the next day or in an hour if they are in pain. At any rate, as long as they want help, we should let them know we are keeping contact.

Then we set about healing ourselves. If we are in public, we can retire to our own quarters or a quiet spot. Then we open ourselves for the experience of release. Perhaps we have to use a mantra or do some positive thinking in order to get our mind quiet, but our goal is not to change anything; it is to experience our own contact with true being. It may take a couple of minutes; it may take hours. If it takes a long time before we really feel a release, perhaps we have to try for a while, break off, and try again later, but we have the responsibility to keep at it until we feel our own rightness. That's all we can do.

Free will enters here. We must have the will to remember the highest truths we know and re-experience what we know. We need to have the will to heal our own belief that there is someone needing healing.

After we have felt our release, that is all we can do. We get up and go about our business. If the problem later pops up again in our consciousness, we must again experience our freedom and repeat the process over and over every time the problem comes into our mind. If the troubled person calls again and still wants help, we sit down once more to check in with reality, but if we feel that all has been taken care of, we would be denying the truth and assuming that we personally had power if we kept on trying.

A man once called me for help, saying he had a backache. I said I would stand by. I went to my room. It took me half an hour to release my belief that I had to help him, that evil was on the field. At any rate, I got my release and went about my business. The next day he called again and said, "It's worse." I said I would continue my work and hung up. Once more I went to my room to check in with the spirit, but right away I had the feeling that there was nothing for me to do. Well, the next day he called again. "It's worse. I can't sleep and my whole back aches now." I asked if he wanted me to continue and he begrudgingly said he did. Once more I checked in, and once more I didn't feel that I had anything to do. My mind kind of wanted to go on thinking something or trying in some way, but I knew I couldn't heal that way, that all I could do was keep myself in tune, so I went about my life.

The next morning, the man called. He said, "Well, that beats all. Last night I got mad. I said, 'That guy isn't going to help me. Nothing is.' And I gave up. Then out of the blue the pain went away and I was free." When he stopped looking for me, a human being, to heal him, when he stopped trying to use mental power, he got his healing.

Actually, the healing took place the first day. That is why I didn't feel any more pull. But the backache was there in order to help the man grow, and when he learned his lesson of growing, it left. The healing was the spiritual principle he learned, not the relief of a backache.

Under grace we are interested in the expansion of

consciousness, in the growth of wholeness, not in patching up bodies or empty purses. Jesus showed us that. He actually healed very few people. He wasn't interested in just making the world a more comfortable place. He was interested in showing humankind its freedom, and at times, by examples of physical healing, he showed that we have in consciousness that which can free the world. But you will notice he healed only those who reached out to him, those who touched him mentally or physically. Once they had touched him, and they had linked up with his consciousness, they were in a position to see his truth work and they were pulled into his wholeness.

When the man at the well asked for healing, Jesus made no emotional or human reaction at all. He simply said, "What's to hinder you? Take up your bed and walk." Jesus was so high that he didn't even see the human illusion of sickness! He saw the true freedom in the man. And by seeing it, the man was lifted into it, lifted right up onto his feet.

Spiritual healing has nothing to do with time or space. A person wanting help can be in Timbuktu; it makes no difference. If he or she makes contact either by telephoning or by writing, or even by sending out mental telegrams, he or she is joined up into the oneness and the work is done.

Our job is to stay in as high a state of consciousness as we can at all times. The more people are looking to us for help, the more responsibility we have to stay high and make contact as often as possible. When there are those who are not even making recognizable contact, but who are reaching out to us in their thoughts, we may not know it, so we have to keep ourselves open. If we feel pulls, someone may be reaching out to us, so we simply recognize that we have to go within and release whatever is causing the pull.

The highest healing state is the one in which a person doesn't even know they are healing anyone, where their presence alone heals, where they leave a trail of lifted people behind them just by the lifting power of their presence.

That is where we will all be one day. One day, when the light has finally chased away all belief in bad and good, we will need no healers and no teachers. All will be hooked together in a lifting vibration, and when one member of the family of mankind starts to lag, the other members will support him just by their presence.

Neither Do I Condemn Thee

The hardest condition to heal is one in which the healer is personally involved. We might find that many, many others reach out to us and that light is brought into their lives, but when it comes to helping the members of our own family, it isn't easy. That's natural and has nothing to do with success or failure.

Our family is part of our own picture. A picture can't jump out of its frame and turn around and see itself. It is easy to see the truth about someone else's family because they are not part of our own picture. When we are personally involved, we have two things to do: one, we give up our own personal responsibility by reaching out for help from others who we feel are good vibrations. Two, we listen within to see if our own problem isn't part of our growth.

Our problem might be the breaking up of old forms so that new ones can come forth. If we halt the apparent disruption, we might be halting progress or growth. But if the disruption is a real disconnect brought on by our ignorance, then it can indeed be healed and lifted. Whether it is our own problem or that of someone who has reached out to us, we must not judge in terms of human good or change involving personal desire.

The minute we judge, the minute we look for results, we are back in the world of law. The minute we are in law, we start condemning some as good and others as bad. Then we see people we know who are mixed up and operating under ignorance, we judge them and cannot heal them.

Whenever we let the slightest judgment enter, whenever we let the slightest feeling of superiority enter, whenever we see those who reach out to us in terms of their failure, we are condemning them, not loving them. Before Jesus healed, he said, "Neither do I condemn thee." That is our motto.   *Judge*

When we look to the life of Jesus for further tips on the spiritual life, or a morality based on grace, we find that he kept telling his followers that they should go heal. The disciples were actually the first revolutionary recruits trying to live by a new morality, and they made the same mistakes we do. When they went out and found that there was indeed something in their consciousness which made healings possible, they came running back to Jesus all puffed up by their accomplishment. But he called a quick halt. He said, in effect, "Now wait a minute; rejoice only that your names are written in heaven."

What is heaven? It is the pure state of wholeness. Heaven is not some place off in the distance. It is right at the spot where we are when we realize our wholeness. The kingdom of heaven is within because we realize our wholeness. As long as we stay in contact with our wholeness, we are welcome to the joy of life itself. That's why we are on the verge of the most joy-filled day the world has ever seen, as man more and more actually realizes his wholeness. As that day grows into fullness, we will have heaven on earth, literally. The world will become a holy place.

The holy place is the holy level of consciousness. We are now passing through the doorway of that place. My friend and teacher, Joel Goldsmith, in his book *The Art of Spiritual Healing*, wrote: "I stand at the doorway of my consciousness, permitting nothing of a discordant nature to enter, maintaining it in its purity as that place through which God flows to all the world. All who enter my spiritual household, my temple, find therein the peace and joy which become the substance of their being, their bodies, or their pocketbooks. This God-consciousness envelops them, governs and sustains them, and reveals this truth as the truth of their own individual being, so that they, in their turn, become a law not only to themselves, but to all who look to them for help.

CHAPTER TEN

The Ultimate Trip
INTO Spirit

My life is an adventure. In terms of my name and my identity, it is a journey into time and space. In terms of consciousness, it is an endless journey into infinity. At best, it is a glorious trip into which I bring my whole self.

From day to day, I have taken many side trips. At one point, I made material success my trip. At another time, the acquirement of human knowledge was my trip. Sometimes making the world a more beautiful place has been my trip, and sometimes I have been on a people trip.

For a while I made sex my trip. For a time I was on a self-indulgence trip. Once, I made the rejection of life itself my trip.

Who is to judge the value or harm of any of my trips? Eventually, and along with all the other trips, as I journeyed the whole map of human existence, I was led to the *ultimate trip*.

The ultimate trip is the journey into spirit. Once I had firmly set my foot on the ultimate trip, all else seemed pale and limited, for all other trips were only facets of the ultimate trip.

Through the ultimate trip I found my love, my purpose, and my life. The ultimate trip is a life lived by grace. It is the life of life and the all of all. It is beyond the judging of all other trips. It does not proselytize. It does not try to lure others into its path by condemning other trips. It simply says, "Let your own light so shine before men that they might see your good works." All mankind is drawn to the light illuminating the ultimate trip.

How do I know when I am on the ultimate trip? Simple. I know because I know what I place at the center of my life. Whatever I place at the center is my trip. I know I do not place money at the center, so I am not on a money trip. I do not place work at the center of my life, so I am not on a work trip. I know I do not place sex at the center, so I am not on a sex trip. I know that food, drink or drugs are not the center. I know I do not think about them or relate everything to them, and whatever I place at the center is that to which I relate. Whatever I relate to is the morning star which guides the ship of my life.

My morning star, the ultimate of ultimates to which I relate, can only be one thing—GOD. God is the ultimate trip. I place God at the center.

Now, I know my heart has always yearned for God. All the other trips have been leading to the ultimate trip. Having once tasted an experience of God, everything else continues to exist, but it exists as a shadow receiving its light from the light of God.

I have found the pearl of great price, and I am willing to sell all I have to buy it. I am willing to offer up my own individual self, the most valuable thing I have, for the ultimate trip. That's the final price.

By paying this price, I have found out a wonderful thing to behold—*I am all that God is*. I am a marvelous thing. I have access to all the heavenly riches. I am beauty and I am love.

Am I willing now to turn around and give even that up? I must, if I want to take the ultimate trip, because the ultimate trip transcends all separateness and merges me into God itself. Like the prodigal son, I came out from God and now I want to return, I want to complete the journey, I want to make the round trip back into the totality of my being-ness from which I came. What must I do to make this last step on the trip?

I must walk the last mile alone. That means that I cannot walk it with the help of any material person, place, or thing. I cannot lean on a teacher, a pill, or any of my personal accomplishments.

Finally, after I have been through all the other trips from which the collective human soul has grown, I stand naked of soul. Then at last I can see an object attracting all souls. In order to lose my final trace of separateness, I must recognize a center at once a part of me and yet apart from me. That is God. God is the center of attraction.

Only by putting God at the center can I experience it and finally merge into it. I must put something bigger than my own consciousness at the center, for just as the leaf has all of the vine within it, the vine is more than the leaf. Just as every cell or organ of my body has a life and activity of its own, I am more than all parts. So, just as all of my fellow humans are cells making up the whole of God, God is both all of us and more than any of us.

When I put God at the center, I can experience it and finally merge into it as others have done. Others before me have washed the world with the light shed from their ultimate trip, and each one of them has said, "I and the father are one, but the father is greater than I." They showed the world by their example that it is possible for me, too—that I have the same potential.

When I realize that Jesus, Buddha, Mohammed, and Rama Krishna proved that man could make the ultimate trip, I know they did it for me because by making the trip themselves they showed me that I can make it. I love them for that.

To realize the very presence of Jesus Christ is to experience him as a living reality. To experience the Christ myself is to experience the possibility of that spiritual evolution which is taking place within me. The love of Jesus Christ is the love of the possibility, the recognition of the possibility.

I must recognize him, and recognizing the possibility in him is the bridge that lifts me totally into his very being and into the totality of God. The evolved accomplished soul of Jesus fills me when I evolve into his fullness, when I accomplish his trip. It is at once me and apart from me, and I can say as Paul did, "I live, yet not I, but Christ in me." Now I and the Father are one.

Now when I pray, it is not I who prays; it is the God within me who prays. My prayer is not my prayer, but it is God praying ME:

I in the midst of the world feed it, clothe it, and house it. I in the midst of you have never been limited. I in the midst of you provides everything necessary to you at all times, for I am not dependent on man who appears separate from me.

I am neither male nor female. I am the *I* which is in all mankind. I am the universal, supreme, divine, true identity of all, no matter what color, race, size, or shape.

I am all. I am the invisible presence in all, showing forth as the many forms of myself. I am the invisible presence which travels through life beside me. I am the life of friend or foe.

I have come that I might have life and that I might have it more abundantly. I have come to fulfill myself, and as you are I, I am fulfilling you when you put me at the center. Now cease from depending on man for your good. Turn to me. Listen to me, the I of your own being. Do not look to effects, do not look for personal power or human protection, for I am living you—I am your very livingness.

You do not have to be a prisoner of fear. You do not have to work your life through in slavery in order to make a living. I am your living. Let go, turn to me, and the prison walls dissolve.

The prison of your body as a limited time-bound and space-bound entity dissolves because your body is a temple of the living God, which I am. I have given you your mind, your body, and your soul. I am all those parts in one. And you are made in my image and likeness, for I am the intelligence which directs the functions of your body, whether this directing is done consciously or unconsciously. I am to you as you are to the parts of your body. Through me you have your life. Therefore the consciousness of your body must be my consciousness. We are one.

Many times you have made false gods, many times you have looked to people and things for life and protections, but always you were really looking for me, for your true self, and didn't know it. You have looked for comfort and pleasure, for peace of mind and affection, and all the time you were looking for me and didn't know it. When you did find peace and joy, it was because you saw me in the world. You felt joy because you felt your own true identity. You learned to look within where I am because I am the I of your being.

Now you know that I am the way, I am the ultimate trip. If you always turn to me, I am there to meet you and show you the way because I am never farther away than you are from yourself, since I am yourself. Your secret place is within your own self. Go into it. Commune with me there. Take sanctuary there.

Trust this I at the center of your very form and being. Trust me. Trust me with all your fears and all your secret desires. Lay them at my feet. I will fulfill you as I always have since the beginning of time.

I am with you now. Don't look back or forward. The only reality is now, the only reality is I. All the help you need will be there when you need it because when it is "now," I will be there, and I am all that you need, for I express myself as friend, companion, food, clothing, shelter, flowers, birds, trees, and all beautiful things.

I am consciousness, and that is all there is, my consciousness. My consciousness is not expressed off in space alone. It is right on earth—all one if there are eyes to see, and I love my creations on earth.

I give myself this prayer:

> *My consciousness which art in earth,*
>   *complete and whole be thy fulfillment.*
>
> *My kingdom come, my will be done*
>   *in the unconscious as it is in the conscious.*
>
> *Give consciousness this day its*
>   *continued expansion.*
>
> *Forgive it its shortcomings as it*
>   *releases me from believing I am finite.*
>
> *Lead it not into confusion*
>   *and deliver it from evil appearance,*
>   *for I AM is the whole, the power,*
>   *and the glory. For ever and ever . . . ALL MEN*

Those who wish to communicate with the author or to receive information about his audio or video recordings, lectures and publications, direct your correspondence to Walter Starcke, Guadalupe Press, Box 865, Boerne, Texas 78006.